ROUTLEDGE LIBRARY EDITIONS:
BANKING & FINANCE

SOMETHING IN THE CITY

SOMETHING IN THE CITY

JOHN BENN

Volume 1

Routledge
Taylor & Francis Group
LONDON AND NEW YORK

First published in 1959

This edition first published in 2012
by Routledge
4 Park Square, Milton Park, Abingdon, Oxon OX14 4RN
605 Third Avenue, New York, NY 10017

Routledge is an imprint of the Taylor & Francis Group, an informa business

British Library Cataloguing in Publication Data
A catalogue record for this book is available from the British Library

ISBN: 978-0-415-52086-7 (Set)
ISBN: 978-0-203-10819-2 (ebk) (Set)
ISBN: 978-0-415-52814-6 (hbk) (Volume 1)
ISBN: 978-0-203-11760-6 (ebk) (Volume 1)

Publisher's Note
The publisher has gone to great lengths to ensure the quality of this reprint but points out that some imperfections in the original copies may be apparent.

Disclaimer
The publisher has made every effort to trace copyright holders and would welcome correspondence from those they have been unable to trace.

Something in the City

JOHN BENN

Ruskin House

GEORGE ALLEN & UNWIN LTD

MUSEUM STREET LONDON

FIRST PUBLISHED IN 1959

PRINTED IN GREAT BRITAIN
in 12pt Bembo type
BY T. AND A. CONSTABLE LTD
EDINBURGH

FOREWORD

More than half a million men and women work in the City of London by day—the night population is only six thousand—but most of them are merely 'Something in the City' to friends and neighbours and very little more to one another. The public at large knows still less about them, and to judge from the critical attitude apparent at the time of the Bank Rate enquiry, when prominent City men were called before a judicial tribunal, many people seem ready to think the worst of those who make a living in the City.

I have therefore written this book with two distinct but complementary objects. The first is to give the general reader, who is assumed to have no direct contact with financial business, an idea of what we do in a City office and Board room, and how we put his money to work. The second object is to encourage the City itself to 'speak up' in what has been aptly termed this loquacious twentieth century. Modesty must be swept aside when big issues are at stake.

It will be obvious to City readers that I have simplified many matters which are in practice very technical, but if Chapters 5-8 should encourage others to put pen to paper in a similar way, they may be helpful to the expert as well as to the layman. The later chapters (9-12), which discuss the impact of politics on business and the need to make our services better known, are primarily addressed to readers in the City and at Westminster, but their argument concerns every one of us, for I shall hope to show that the best interests of the City and the public are identical.

Throughout the book there are references to the United States, as the City and Wall Street are in constant touch and a great deal of British capital is now invested there. Crossing the

Atlantic is always a tonic, and now that the *Comet* makes the flight in six hours these links will become still closer.

Not without hesitation I have included some personal history, in order to show why I am able to view the City of London with more detachment than those who have worked there all their lives. While based to some extent on the business of the United Kingdom Provident Institution, an insurance office founded in 1840, this book does not commit the Institution or my colleagues in any other companies in any way.

I am indebted to the authors of several other books on the City, to whom acknowledgments are made in later pages; and to a number of friends for helpful advice and assistance, especially Lord Latymer, Mr Basil Tripp and my secretary, Miss Rose Reeves.

Limpsfield J. B.
November 1958

CONTENTS

ILLUSTRATIONS

I

THE DAILY ROUND

I

First Impressions

Fleet Street and Gracechurch Street are both in the City of London, each is a focal point of world-wide activity, but they might be in different planets. When, some ten years ago, I migrated from one to the other, I was immediately struck by the air of reticence in my new surroundings. Having been brought up to believe that it 'pays to advertise', one is surprised to find that stockbrokers are strictly forbidden to cry their wares, and that most people in the City, like the members of the professions, say very little about their work. Obviously, bankers must respect the confidences of their customers, and underwriters often insure risks which are of intimate concern. But many other trades have no such limitations, and while I learned that the City's overseas earnings were paying for nearly a third of the food imported into the United Kingdom, the whole atmosphere in this highly romantic place of business was almost one of apology.

In May, 1949, the senior officials of an insurance company were advised that the Board had appointed me to succeed my father as chairman. Although I had been a director for eight years, the invitation had come as a complete surprise. My main occupation was publishing, and I had never thought of abandoning this fascinating business. But the new appointment offered wide opportunities and it had a political aspect which strongly appealed to me. It happened that insurance was then being talked about as a candidate for nationalization, and having contested the General Election of 1945 I had given a good deal of thought to an issue likely to loom larger in the future. A Labour Government was bent on further plans affecting finance, in every way politics was impinging more and more on business, and for any student of affairs the City offered exciting prospects.

On the first morning in my new office, my desk was piled high with memoranda, everyone wanting to put me in the picture; and at once the general manager arranged a tour of the departments which, in the intervals of other work, was to occupy several weeks while I was getting the measure of new colleagues and surroundings. To judge from my diary there was plenty of variety, and as usually happens, the trivial and the significant combined to keep me well occupied.

June 28 Talked with surveyor and stock exchange manager about investment proposals for the Board tomorrow.

Evening: Annual meeting of local housing association, and two hours' homework.

June 29 Took first Board Meeting. Well rehearsed and went smoothly. Grateful for directors' consideration in refraining from questions on detail.

July 1 Investment Committee: almost a full muster of the Board, with economic adviser in attendance.

Explored adjoining property, a century old, earmarked for rebuilding: ground floor occupied by our staff, remainder a labyrinth of tenants.

July 4 Long session with the agency manager, who is responsible for branches all over the country.

Attended weekly conference presided over by senior medical officer, at which border-line and doubtful cases are discussed.

July 7 Met staff of associated company. Impressed by excellent organization of a young concern untrammelled by tradition.

Afternoon: Editor of *Electrical Journal* called to relate experience since nationalization of electricity and how companies had reacted to the change.

July 8 Board Committee.

July 12 Call from senior partner in G. & Co., who invite us to underwrite the new issue of Messrs L. Also discussed need for publicity for the City.

All evening prepared for Board.

July 13 Second Board Meeting: heavy going, on an exceptionally hot day. Wide differences of view on property investment proposals, but got through thanks to intensive homework.

July 14 To Fleet Street to deal with proofs of a book I had initiated some months ago. Experienced inevitable nostalgia for old job.

In the autumn I began a series of visits to the branch offices, which took me all over the country. Each visit invariably proved a tonic, as the enthusiasm of the field staff was infectious; it is always a good thing to see the problems of a business through the eyes of the men who are in direct touch with the public. I was taken round Dublin by a director of another insurance company who drove me to Phoenix Park in a small car with a large dog, which insisted on licking my ears from the back seat. In Bristol I chanced upon a second-hand copy of *A Trip Round the World*, by W. S. Caine, who as chairman of our Institution in 1900 had made the grand tour first-class for £300.

One other diary entry recalls a conversation with a director who has since retired. He told me that in his early days he was supplied with a new quill pen at every Board meeting, a practice which dated from 1840.

And this brings me to the first Board at which I presided. Fortunately for a new chairman the proceedings follow a well-established order; under the friendly eye of the Secretary, other executives are called into the Board room to provide expert opinions, and the respect traditionally accorded to the chair is a great help.

In calling upon a director for his views on a particular item, I soon felt like an organist handling the stops—pulling one out to encourage a modest colleague, pushing another in when an opinion was overstated. Viewed from the chair, it was quickly apparent how much our discussions gained from the experience of part-time directors, whose functions I shall describe in a later chapter. One of our bankers could always be counted on for the right advice on the trend of the gilt-edged market. In the case of industrial investments, a colleague who is also a manufacturer would often know the firm concerned at first hand from his extensive travels, and his acquaintance with the engineering industry was of particular value. Another director, a retired diplomat, would weigh in with political comments, although he was not always given the hearing he deserved, doubtless because Boards are not immune from the impatience which politics are apt to arouse even in the best-regulated circles. A colleague whose experience had been gained outside the City would sometimes press his views with surprising confidence and the stops had to be applied, but the great sense of unity in the Board room helped us to get through a full agenda in the brief space of an hour.

The main responsibility of the directors of a life assurance company is to look after the very large funds which it must hold. A person who insures his life agrees to pay an annual premium to secure a capital sum when his policy matures. In the case of an endowment assurance this sum is payable after a specified number of years (or on death, if earlier), and in the case of a whole-life policy it is paid on death. In either case, if it is a with-profit policy the original sum assured may be increased by as much as 50 per cent. The successful investment of the premiums is therefore of the first importance to the policyholder as well as to the company, whose competitive position is largely determined by the rate of profit earned and the resultant bonus which is usually declared every three or five years.

As was perhaps to be expected from a new broom, soon after my appointment I began to review our investment policy with a Committee of the Board. We had various aims in mind, for example to increase our holdings of preference shares and to alter the proportions of the funds invested in various classes of stock. In practice these aims were largely upset by political factors: certain risks attaching to the repayment of preference shares had been aggravated by recent Court decisions; dividend limitation had led us to regard the margin of earnings over the rate of interest paid as the important factor, and so on. We decided to reduce some investments in order to limit our stake in any one concern and to effect a wider spread. In making a large-scale review of this sort, the temptation to exchange shares merely for the sake of change had to be resisted, bearing in mind the expense and detailed work involved in Stock Exchange transactions; and we were of course aware that many shares offered to us in the normal course of business would not satisfy any rigid formula, however carefully devised.

After these preliminary discussions, which occupied several meetings, we set out to review the whole Stock Exchange portfolio by the end of 1950, when our assets were next due to be valued. With the help and advice of the investment managers we succeeded in carrying out this intensive programme, which afforded a fascinating picture of investment practice and problems. Listening to the views of my colleagues, some of whom had spent a lifetime in finance, I came to appreciate the trained and almost instinctive judgment of the City, and how much the man in the street—in our case the holder of an insurance policy—owes to the 'know how', based on generations of experience, which plays such an important part in our daily work. Its incalculable value to the national economy will be discussed in a later chapter.

* * * * *

Another first impression brought out during the discussion of investments was the diverse and colourful character of the City's business. There is so much more to it than the figures which loom so large in the popular mind but are merely symbols of countless activities all over the world. Something of this romance was revealed during the Festival of Britain, when for a few sunny weeks, forgetting the rigours of the early post-war years, the City opened its doors to the man in the street. Lloyd's produced a replica of the original coffee shop where marine underwriting was instituted in the eighteenth century. The Livery Companies, notably the Goldsmiths, displayed many of their treasures. The Council of the Stock Exchange was already briefing the public on the mysteries of what Tony Weller called the 'things that go up and down in the City', and set an example since followed by the 'Big Five' which are now reminding us of the varied services offered by the banks. In the past few years this kind of advertisement has spread, but for a city whose business runs into thousands of millions the amount spent in this way is negligible.

By and large, the City still works in silence. This may not have mattered when affairs were in the hands of those whom Sir David Kelly, in a diplomatic context, has termed the Ruling Few. But now that we are all minding each other's business, and every established institution is liable to attention from Parliament, it is time to shed our remaining inhibitions and explain ourselves to the Ruling Many. This will not be easy; some of the City's business is very technical, and I recall that Mr Harold Wincott, whose articles enliven the *Financial Times* on Tuesdays, described a foreign exchange dealer's office during a busy spell as 'the nearest thing to Bedlam' he had ever met. But even so, we still use a lot of unnecessary jargon which helps to confuse and mislead the public. In consequence, many people tend to think of the City chiefly in terms of making and losing vast sums of money, usually—according to the sensational newspapers—in a few hours. Very often, of course, only a fraction of the shares concerned change hands for cash, and the fact that fluctuations in value are largely on paper is seldom appreciated. I soon learned that the large figures with which the

City is popularly associated usually represent many small transactions whose benefits are widely shared. I also became conscious of professional standards established long before the present generation came on the scene, and which will be maintained, I feel sure, by many generations to come. 'The silk hat is not the badge of plutocracy it is often represented to be', I remarked in 1950 to my policyholders, 'nor are the silver buttons of our messengers a sign of subservience. The silk hat was worn originally because it was easily raised to the customer, but it is also, like the buttons, symbolic of the strict and exact standards which happily still mark the business of the City. This is perhaps most clearly recognized abroad, especially in the United States, where a reputation built up over many years is still our most valuable asset.'

As a newcomer to the City I was also struck by the absolute confidence placed in the spoken word. 'Where a nod is as good as a contract' was the apt title given to a recent press photograph of the crowded floor of the Stock Exchange, and this description could be applied to many other activities. The Discount Market, which collects any cash not for the moment being used by one bank or institution and lends it to another on what is termed 'short call', deals in millions of pounds every day largely by word of mouth. It goes without saying that the terms of investment transactions arranged over the telephone are never questioned later, except on the very rare occasions when a clerical mistake occurs. Nowhere in the world, I imagine, is so much business done so quickly and with so little paper as in the City of London.

2

'Ships, Towers, Domes'

Walking over London Bridge I seldom fail to enjoy the first glimpse of the City, especially on a sunny morning when the clouds race above Adelaide House, and at the quay below a ship prepares to sail for Norway or Spain. Some lines written on Westminster Bridge in 1802 would then have been equally descriptive of this other scene:

> 'This City now doth like a garment wear
> the beauty of the morning: silent, bare,
> Ships, towers, domes . . .'

Wordsworth would have had a clear view of the church of St Magnus Martyr and of the Monument, as the road from the old bridge ran directly past the church and up Fish Street Hill. He would also have seen the spires of St Benet Gracechurch, St Margaret Pattens and St Dunstan-in-the-East, another Wren church of great beauty still completely visible from the bridge. But now we can only just see the tower of St Magnus Martyr above Adelaide House, which is taller than the original building named in 1835 after Queen Adelaide, the wife of William IV, 'the Sailor King'. As a boy I must sometimes have passed this building, since it was not demolished until 1921, but I did not then connect it with my present business, which had offices there for more than half a century. Earlier generations of the staff looked from the windows at the frequent processions, in which the Victorians delighted: the *Illustrated London News* of 1863 shows a stand erected outside our office for the State entry into the City of Princess Alexandra of Denmark, a few days before her marriage to Edward, Prince of Wales. During Queen Victoria's Diamond Jubilee celebrations in 1897 the staff were treated to an unrehearsed spectacle when the Duke of Westminster, who was riding behind the Queen's carriage, fell off his horse just as the procession passed our building.

At that time a drinking fountain was a feature of Adelaide Place. A meeting of our policyholders held in May, 1859, had resolved that 'a sum not exceeding £100 be placed at the disposal of the directors for the erection of a drinking fountain in front of the offices', and a contemporary newspaper hoped that this example would be followed by other insurance companies which 'have a *special* interest in promoting habits of sobriety and industry among all classes'. According to the same journal, more lives proposed for insurance were then rejected on account of intemperance than any other cause, but whatever the motives for providing the fountain—and publicity may have been one of them—the completion of the project called for as much patience as it would require today. The Board minutes of 1860 refer to 'difficulties and delay' and record that 'numerous applications had to be made to the City authorities for permission to erect the fountain . . . many months elapsed before leave was finally given and the design approved'.

Five years later the Secretary was instructed to find out how many people used the fountain over a period of twenty-four hours, and he reported that between 7 a.m. of June 14, 1865, and 7 a.m. the following morning, 3,176 people had refreshed themselves there. This is an astonishing figure, and yet it is recorded without comment in the minute book. It means that more than two people drank there every minute of the twenty-four hours, so that if we allow for some slackening-off during the night, we must envisage a queue all through the day. Perhaps the day of the count was unusually hot! However, a wood-cut of the fountain shows that two or three jets of water flowed into a large basin from which several persons could drink at once by cupping the water in their hands. The mystery is further explained if we recall that in those days there were no popular restaurants of any kind other than public houses, and so a drinking fountain would fill a very real need on such a busy thoroughfare as London Bridge.

Ten years later the fountain had had so much hard use that, not for the first time, it was in need of repair. Instead of this, the directors resolved to erect a new one 'of an improved character', which included a bronze group consisting of a girl giving a cup of water to an old man. The new fountain was formally opened by the Lord Mayor and Lady Mayoress on October 28, 1884, but its stay was a short one. After a few years it was found that the great weight of the fountain was causing cracks to appear in the arches of the warehouses beneath the road, so the Board eventually, although sadly, decided to remove it to Clapham Common. And there it may still be seen, a good example of the public design of its period and an honourable relic of Victorian enterprise.

* * * * *

I must not, of course, suggest that most of us who work in the City give much thought to its history, yet if we take a bus to Aldgate we are at once stepping into the distant past, for this was one of the gates in our equally familiar London Wall built round the City by the Romans, part of which still stands near the Tower of London. The others were Newgate, Cripplegate, Bishopsgate and Ludgate.

The City had its origins at the first bridgable but still navigable stretch of the Thames. Tacitus described a Celtic first-century settlement as 'celebrated for the gathering of dealers and commodities', and for 2,000 years the City's business has been bound up with ships. In the eleventh century a tariff for vessels entering London was introduced to raise revenues for the King's Exchequer: a small ship coming to Billingsgate paid a toll of a halfpenny, a larger vessel paid a penny, and a full-sized ship fourpence. This tax could also be paid in kind, a captain with a cargo of planks having to surrender one plank as toll, just as at that time the farmers who brought chickens to the London markets had to give one hen for every basketful carried on a pack-horse. At a later date the crews of a wine fleet coming from Germany sang a hymn on arriving in the Thames, as a thanksgiving for having escaped the perils of the Channel. They then moored near London Bridge, and one of the City Sheriffs and the King's Chamberlain boarded each ship to 'select for the royal use such articles as they might think proper'. Evidently taxation was then a simpler form of exaction than it is today.

I wonder how many of those who now lunch at the Savoy realize that the hotel stands on the site of the Earl of Savoy's mansion built in 1245. At that time the noblemen made their homes on the marshy banks of the river between the City, dominated by St Paul's, and Westminster with its famous Abbey. Another familiar building, the Royal

Exchange, was put up in 1566 as a meeting place for merchants who came to the City from many places abroad; trade with the Continent developed rapidly when wool was sent to the Low Countries in exchange for fine cloth, wine and spices. A century later the original Exchange was destroyed in the Great Fire of London and rebuilt, and was finally replaced in 1844 by the present unattractive building opposite the Bank of England.

In the development of the City as we know it today, the coffee houses played an important part; not long ago a plaque was put up in St Michael's Alley, Cornhill, to commemorate the opening of the first of them three hundred years ago. Its proprietor, Daniel Edwards, was a great traveller. He had brought home a supply of coffee from Smyrna, together with a Greek servant to prepare it for him. We read that coffee was at first hailed as a remedy for all complaints but quickly caught on as a popular drink, and coffee shops then sprang up under the signs of the Rainbow, the Sultan Solyman and so on. They soon became centres for talk on politics and philosophy as well as business, so much so that Macaulay wrote that 'the coffee house was the Londoner's home and those who wished to find a gentleman commonly asked not whether he lived in Fleet Street or Chancery Lane but whether he frequented the Grecian or the Rainbow'. A penny was paid for admission and the coffee houses became known as the 'penny universities'. As I shall mention in a later chapter on the Stock Exchange, its messengers are still called waiters because its business was first transacted in the then novel coffee houses, and the same applied to Lloyd's, where British marine insurance originated.

Lloyd's coffee house was first opened in Tower Street in

1687 and later moved to Lombard Street, and gave its name to the largest institution in the world for insuring ships and cargoes. On receipt of news, it was the custom for a youth to 'get into the pulpit and read every paper with a loud and distinct voice while the audience are sipping their respective liquors'—I quote from the *Tatler* of December, 1710. The modern counterpart of the pulpit is the rostrum from which a waiter calls the names of members who are wanted, and announces important news by sounding the Lutine Bell, two strokes for good news, one for bad. The bell came from a French frigate named the *Lutine*, which, after capture by the Royal Navy, was wrecked off the Dutch coast in 1799 with nearly one million pounds worth of gold on board; needless to say, Lloyd's paid the insurance claim promptly. The bell and rudder were later salvaged, the rudder being made into a chair and table.

In 1813, Lloyd's insured the life of Napoleon Bonaparte. In 1957, when *Mayflower II* sailed across the Atlantic on the route of the Pilgrim Fathers, it provided the policy which was written on parchment in the form issued in 1620 when the original *Mayflower* set out on her voyage.

From the start Lloyd's exhibited a characteristic of the City to which I shall often refer in this book: its business has always depended on individual liability, which still distinguishes it from almost every other place of insurance in the world. When a shipowner or a householder insures in this market, he places his risk not with the Corporation of Lloyd's but with one or more syndicates of underwriters. Every member of a syndicate is directly liable to the policyholder for his share of any loss that may fall on the policy on which the number of his syndicate appears. At one time underwriters carried on their business singly and each man accepted risks for himself and himself only. I am told that if that method had been continued, the great development of the last fifty years would not have been possible, but fortunately the syndicate system grew up, enabling agents to deal in much larger sums than before and enormously widening their scope.

Besides the underwriter, the broker who acts as the agent of the policyholder plays a key part. His duty is to represent the assured, to put his risks before the underwriters as favourably as possible and to obtain the best terms when the insurance is placed. If there should be a claim, the broker also arranges the settlement, collects the money and pays it out. He must select the most suitable underwriters for each risk, know enough of the law to secure the contract in its right form and generally act as guide, philosopher and friend to his clients. As Lloyd's draws its business from every continent and most countries, it follows that the brokers' connections are cast very wide; wherever free enterprise is permitted, there are few places in which it is not possible to find firms or individuals with contacts for placing marine, fire and accident business in London. While Lloyd's handles the bulk of the marine business, an even larger volume of general insurance is dealt with by the great insurance companies, whose story I shall touch on later in this book.

* * * * *

In earlier times, before the commercial buildings began to dominate the City, the many masts of ships must have vied with the church spires on the skyline, to underline the fact that London is first and foremost a centre of world-wide trade.

From its offices in the City the famous East India Company

laid the foundations of the Indian Empire, and in the same way the Hudson's Bay Company opened up Canada, where it still does an enormous business from its headquarters at Beaver Hall. The Company displayed 250 kinds of fur skins during the Festival of Britain, and through the auctions held regularly, London is still the international fur centre of the world. Tea, wool, rubber, metals are other commodities dealt with as part of our daily business. The markets are found in Mincing Lane, Fenchurch Street and Eastcheap, which converge upon the Pool of London. The Metal Exchange will sell tin from Malaya to the United States, Canada may bid for rubber on the London Commodity Exchange at Plantation House, and Belgians may buy Australian wool through London—the Wool Exchange is in Coleman Street. As I have already mentioned, all this 'third party' trade comes to us because foreigners trust the City and have dealt with us for generations.

Some of this trade is in 'futures', that is in commodities which will not be available for some months ahead. As the name implies, London dealers buy such commodities in advance, making a living by gauging the likely demand and prices that will prevail when the commodities are available. Meanwhile, planters and wool growers and owners of mines are assured of a market, and are able to plan their crops and production accordingly. Other commodities which help to swell the enormous international earnings of the City are tin, copper, lead and zinc, gold, silver and diamonds.

In this quick look round the City I next come to St Mary Axe, where the Baltic and Mercantile Shipping Exchange is located. Like Lloyd's, this exchange originated in the coffee houses of the eighteenth century and now handles air freights as well as shipping, both important sources of so-called 'invisible' earnings. As I shall show in another chapter, shipping and insurance both earn money overseas without calling for corresponding physical or 'visible' exports, and so help to pay for a substantial part of the goods and commodities we are obliged to import. The modern shipping broker handles world-wide transport needs, and from his office in London arranges for cargoes of all kinds to be shipped from one country to another.

From all this it follows that London has the largest port in the world, although it needs to be emphasized that only a small proportion of the goods that are bought and sold in the City ever cross its boundaries or come within miles of it. The wealth of the City is in fact derived from an extensive combination of trading and financial services which have no precise counterpart in any other place in the world. Sir Oscar Hobson, the doyen of the City editors, explains in *How The City Works* that the topographical arrangement of our institutions and markets is not the result of mere accident but has an important bearing on their mutual working. What is known as the 'square mile' is not, in fact, square at all. It is of an irregular crescent shape extending from the Temple through Finsbury to Aldgate. The heart of the City is in the smaller area which has the Bank of England as its centre, and around this area the various commodity markets are grouped, each specializing in its own type of business. These markets adjoin the 'inner banking-Stock Exchange-insurance quarter' because the services provided from that quarter are absolutely essential to their efficiency. In the normal course of business much of the money that makes possible the world-wide movement of goods has to be borrowed, and with the immense resources at its command, the City provides that money and so keeps the wheels turning. The City furnishes 'a mechanism by which payment of any sum of money, large or small, may be made with safety and despatch, without the use of actual notes or coin'. This in turn 'enables foodstuffs and raw materials to be produced, to be transported about the world and to undergo processes of manufacture until they are finally sold as finished, consumable articles'.

Working in the City I am constantly reminded that money is a commodity like any other, and that figures are simply a measure of transactions in goods and services of many kinds. This was easier to grasp when Britain was on the gold standard, but there is a reminder of the underlying nature of money in the wind vane which still stands in the Court Room of the Bank of England. In the days of sailing-ships the vane showed the bankers how the ships bound for the port of London were progressing and so enabled them to judge how soon payment for the cargoes would be required. Although, in this more complex age, we are inclined to think in vague terms of International Monetary Funds, European Payment Unions, and the like, the necessity for our island people to 'find the money' for imported food and raw materials is as pressing as ever; the ships that dock below London Bridge today are no less vital to the country than were the sailing-ships which graced the Thames a century ago.

This brings me again to London Bridge and the original Adelaide House, a view of which is preserved in my present offices in Gracechurch Street. When we added a wing to the building in 1957 the Board commissioned Mr C. Walter Hodges to provide a picture for the new entrance hall, and I greatly enjoyed looking into the historical details with this distinguished artist. Describing his painting as 'a wide and exciting panorama of ships and towers and streets and people of a hundred years ago', Mr Hodges has answered in his pamphlet, *It Began with a Fountain*, two questions on its composition which deserve to be quoted, as they explain what some of us feel about the continuity of our work in the City. The artist has shown, in the foreground, a young man losing some papers over London Bridge—they are fluttering in the breeze to the river below—and a group of prosperous Victorians also faces the spectator. 'I have heard it suggested,' Mr Hodges comments, 'though goodness knows why, that this man is throwing his insurance policies away. Others have supposed that he is an enthusiastic social reformer trying to distribute pamphlets to the crew of the paddleboat below. But the truth is that he is a martyr to artistic composition, and that this everlasting loss of his papers has been forced upon him, all unbeknown to himself, in order that the artist might have a means of counteracting, by a flutter of papers, the over-strong directional lines of the bridge, which run in the opposite direction. And the second question is: "What are all the other people looking at?" The answer to the spectator is: "They are looking at you. The Past is looking to the Future as the Future looks to the Past". *Quoniam sumus in vicem membra.*'

3

An Adventurous Business

The gilded signs that hang in Lombard Street make this one of the most colourful streets in the City. It includes the Church of St Edmund the King and Martyr built in 1690 and, down the adjoining alley, the fine building in Georgian style put up for Williams Deacon's Bank in 1936. Like the barbers' poles which were a feature of mediaeval London, the anchors, the seashells and the mermaids still tell us of the trades carried on in this busy thoroughfare. Some of these signs date from 1902, when leading merchant and banking houses provided new signs for the Coronation of King Edward VII. Others were added in 1911 when King George V was crowned, and Martins Bank then put up a gilded grasshopper. Not long after its appearance two draymen were heard discussing this giant insect.

'What's that?' one of them enquired.

'Their trademark, of course,' replied the other; 'a blood-sucker!'

Inspired by these many impressive signs, I decided in 1950 to display a similar device on our offices in Gracechurch Street and for this purpose Robert Herrick was commissioned to design a sundial. We had moved our headquarters from the Strand to this present new address in 1941, when the bomb which virtually destroyed the Church of St Clement Danes also damaged nearby buildings too severely for continued occupation. Altogether no fewer than twenty City churches were destroyed during the war, many during the second great fire of London which occurred on the night of December 29, 1940. Although St Paul's emerged unscathed, the adjoining Paternoster Row went up in flames, together with stocks of books, mainly religious, valued at over £3,000,000.

In those trying days and in the early post-war years, City workers found consolation in the herbs and flowers which quickly sprang up amid the ruins. During the war I cut out of a copy of *The Spectator* an article on the works of John Gerard, a herbalist who had a house in Holborn and an orchard in Chancery Lane, where he grew (among other things) what was called the 'exotic potato plant from Virginia'. Gerard found wild herbs in mediaeval London—bugloss in Piccadilly, pennywort at Westminster Abbey, willow herb on Thames Bank. 'Our enemies', wrote Miss Phyllis Giles, 'would make mock of the fact that the grass was growing in the streets of London, but to us the green shoots are promises of healing, descendants from a great past and symbols of resurrection.'

The great rebuilding programme which is now being carried out in the City got off from rather a slow start, due to the priorities necessarily given to housing, and to the many restrictions we have had to satisfy since 1945 relating to finance as well as architecture. About 27 million square feet of floor space were destroyed during the war and the reconstruction of a great part of this vast area is now in hand. The work includes the restoration of the Temple, fifteen Livery halls, Guildhall and eighteen City churches, while many new and impressive blocks of offices have now been erected.

All this activity recalls the earlier wave of construction that followed the Great Fire of 1666, when Barbon, who was a son of Praise-God Barebones of Cromwell's Parliament, opened a fire insurance office in 1680 and so started a business which has grown to immense dimensions throughout the world. The Phoenix office soon followed, and firemarks were then fixed to buildings insured by this and other companies. They kept their own fire brigades, and when a fire occurred, it could be seen from the firemarks which office was responsible for putting it out. It is alleged that sometimes a brigade, finding a competitor's firemark on a building in flames, left it to burn; perhaps there were occasions when it extinguished the fire and solicited the insurance afterwards!

* * * * *

Most people look upon insurance as a dry-as-dust business in which we spend our days making calculations so complex that few can understand them. In fact, from the beginning insurance has been an adventurous business; a Statute of Queen Elizabeth I, dated 1601, gave us a definition which has stood the test of time:

> 'By means of a policy of assurance it cometh to pass that upon the loss or perishing of any ship there followeth not the undoing of any man but the loss lighteth rather easily upon many than heavily upon few.'

The Statute adds: 'whereby merchants, especially the younger sort, are allured to adventure more willingly and more freely'. This is still the keynote of insurance.

The earliest known marine policy to be drawn up in English was written in 1555 and, as already mentioned, fire insurance followed a century later. Life assurance began in Britain in 1721, when the Royal Exchange and London Assurance companies were founded. Actually, the Company of Parish Clerks in the City of London had started to keep weekly records of baptisms and burials at a much earlier date, but an attempt to institute life assurance by the Mercers Company broke down, despite the vast resources of this great City Guild, because they made scarcely any distinctions between the ages and state of health of those admitted—personal and individual factors that still play an important part in insurance business. The early science of life assurance owed much to Edmond Halley, the astronomer, and the foundations were laid when the Equitable Society obtained its Charter in 1761.

In the previous chapter I have described the Corporation of Lloyd's, and the term 'A 1 at Lloyd's' has long been the hallmark of sound shipping throughout the world. Coming to the nineteenth century, the establishment of railways gave rise to accident insurance, now embracing motor insurance. The invention of steam led to the foundation of specialist companies insuring against boiler explosion, this in turn developing into the whole range of modern engineering insurance, lately extended to atomic energy risks. Aviation insurance, dating from 1912, is going ahead by leaps and bounds, all of which shows that insurance in our free society is constantly being adapted and extended to new needs. Giving all the credit due to the inventors, it is no exaggeration to say that without insurance the greater part of modern trade and industry would not have been promoted and developed.

From the earliest days British insurance companies have been allured by the prospects of adventure overseas. They gained a footing in Canada in 1807, in India about 1820, in America in the forties, and in Australia before the famous 'gold rush' of 1851. It is said that when the American Civil War ended, a former general, who was also the agent for a British insurance company, rode across the country settling claims from bags of gold tied to his saddle! Disastrous fires which destroyed pioneer towns in Newfoundland and in the West Indies were paid for by British insurers, without whose backing the victims would have lost everything.

The variety of risks now insured in London is fascinating. An American inventor recently insured a model typewriter with a Chinese keyboard on its journey from New York to Shanghai for $50,000; the stock of a bird's nest soup dealer in Hong Kong is insured in London. In Malaya a British cash-in-transit policy covers the risk of loss of cash, which is dropped from an aeroplane for the wages of six or seven rubber estates in order to avoid the hazardous journey by road. Cash at race meetings in Canada is insured in London against theft, so is the liability risk on an amusement park in Israel. British underwriters now cover a chain of shops in Holland, the terms of the policy protecting the owners against damage from riot and 'roguery'. In contrast with the unfortunate step taken by the British nationalized airways in removing the British flag from our aircraft, a British insurance company operating motor insurance in Brazil issues its policyholders with a card bearing the Union Jack, and Brazilians show these cards to their friends to emphasize how wise they are to 'insure British'.

No wonder! There has been no recorded case of a British insurance company failing to pay a just claim in any part of the world. Our Governments have always allowed exchange for the settlement of claims. There are good reasons for this. Insurance is a most valuable export; the overseas premium income from the fire, accident and marine business of all British insurers now amounts to about £900 million a year. The net earnings average about £50 million, not as much as from cars or textiles but, since insurance involves no raw materials or shipping space, and much less manpower, it also can be classed as a major exporting business. A City worker is therefore just as productive as, say, an engineer, a fact which I find is news to most people. The annual premium income of the British insurance market, including life business, now adds up to about £1,650 million, of which nearly £1,350 million is attributable to the companies and the balance to Lloyd's. The companies' income alone averages £4 million per day, but I want to emphasize that all these figures are in the main the sum of many little ones. Every figure represents some personal transaction, associated with the work and achievement and ambitions of individuals in many parts of the world.

* * * * *

Just the same thing is true of the work that goes on, day by day, in the affairs of a life office at home. All over the country our branch offices are seeking new assurances and are giving service to existing policyholders and agents.

In the course of the year the field staff of my Institution travels 700,000 miles, and their experiences would fill a book. A recent enquiry from an officer serving on board a ship took one of our managers to sea in a rowing-boat and he secured a proposal while his soaking wet clothes were being dried in the cook's galley. In another case, the cheque for the first premium was signed on the deck of a liner five minutes before a tea planter sailed for India. One of our staff secured a policy from a farmer at milking time by offering to milk a cow, and doing this to the farmer's complete satisfaction while he filled in the proposal form. As if to go one better, another inspector helped to bring some lambs into the world in Derbyshire! I must not suggest that such adventures are a daily occurrence; most life policies involve careful negotiation over long periods, during which friendship and confidence are slowly but firmly built up, but for the field staff the unexpected is always just round the corner. Once a proposal for assurance has been secured, a great deal of work ensues at the head office, and in describing this I must ask the reader to put up with some more figures. Without these, it is impossible to visualize what a lot of detail the daily round in the City involves.

More than 10,000 proposals reach us from all parts of the United Kingdom every year, and about 3,000 examinations are carried out by our medical officers, who must assess all kinds of occupational risks. In addition to the work involved in writing new policies, the changing needs of members require 4,500 endorsements to existing contracts.

Premium rates are carried by the field staff in a loose-leaf book, and as there are some 8,000 separate rates, any change presents a task of monumental proportions. The types of policy we issue range from the traditional assurance payable only on death, to the mortgage protection policy introduced to cover the outstanding amount under building society contracts. Requests for special rates are varied and sometimes unusual: for example, a lady of ninety recently required a temporary assurance for two weeks, while at the other extreme we quoted for whole-life policies for a boy and a girl each under the age of ten.

We offer loans on the security of policies, and about 12,000 quotations for loans, surrender values and paid-up policy values are issued annually. In addition to these direct services to members, the actuarial department does a large amount of statistical work, the main task being the calculation of our liabilities. This is now largely mechanized, but the problems of maintaining the policy card index are considerable, and one year's movements may involve nearly a tenth of the file. At the end of every third year this work has an added significance when the bonuses are declared. Although there were 87,000 participating policies in force at the last declaration and each bonus was calculated in duplicate in the interests of accuracy, this heavy duty was completed, chiefly after office hours, in seven weeks. The staff which deals with pensions business has to be constantly on the watch for new legislation and, more often, for changes in Inland Revenue practice which affect existing regulations.

Of the many statistics relating to the insurance business, I am always fascinated by the fact that over 7,000 changes of address are notified to us annually, and as we are only one of eighty offices this gives some idea of the constant movement of the population in the British Isles. We issue 90,000 renewal notices every year. These are matched by incoming remittances, and in addition 19,000 premiums are paid monthly by banker's order.

Every insurance company receives an occasional complaint about claims, but in life assurance few cases present any difficulty. The aim is to pay the correct amount to the correct person as soon as possible and with the least formality consistent with prudence. In 1957 payments of about

£3,000,000 were made, many under small policies, while the granting and repayment of loans and the registration of notices of assignment involved another 5,000 transactions. Such matters as the relation of the Married Women's Property Act to Estate Duty and the investigation of title to policies are all in the day's work.

At some point or another, most of the processes I have described concern our accounting organization, whose staff has not only to produce accounts but must render returns and fulfil the conditions of the various Acts of Parliament governing our business. It also has to supply the directors with regular information, and to exercise a financial control over all departments, branches, agents and others who handle monies due by or to the Institution. Besides the books and ledgers relating to life assurance itself, there are the accounts of our Stock Exchange securities, properties, ground rents, mortgages and policy loans—comprising nearly 14,000 investments from which interest now exceeding £2,900,000 a year has to be collected. The total cash received and paid out by the Institution during 1957 was over £30,000,000. Within a few weeks of closing the books on December 31, all these sums had been sorted into their correct pigeon-holes, the ledgers balanced, and finally a year's work had been condensed into the few lines which make up the revenue account and balance sheet in the annual report.

To complete this picture of the work of an insurance head office, I must include a reference to the investment departments, which deal every day with the Stock Exchange and property markets. The actual investment is only part of the business: company reports are coming in all the time and have to be studied; records and charts must be kept up to date; a mass of other detail requires continuous attention.

Authority for making investments rests with the Board of directors, who will discuss with equal thoroughness a proposal to invest £5,000 or £500,000—and this careful process is going on, to the advantage of those who insure and of those who look to us for capital, in many City Board rooms every week.

* * * * *

What takes place at a typical Board meeting? What precisely do we talk about? Twelve directors, the Secretary, and the Accountant are sitting at the Board table, and at noon we hear the minutes of the previous meeting.

'The minutes having been read, is it your pleasure they be signed?' The Secretary hands me the minute book and to a murmur of 'agreed' from the directors I add my signature to the page. Another Board meeting has begun. I refer to the formal proceedings, because during the previous half an hour or so the directors have been signing cheques and policies and other documents. Sometimes this work is not quite finished when the meeting begins, and the scratching of pens is heard in a minor key while the minutes are being read out.

Next, the Accountant presents the Bank Statement and informs us that after allowing for uncleared cheques there is a balance of £50,000 on current account, or it may be £200,000, depending on the time of the month. Occasionally we are overdrawn, but, whatever the figure, it is some guide to the extent of the investments to be considered later in the meeting.

I proceed to move that the seal of the Company be affixed to various documents: first, of course, to assurance policies; then to a deed of licence and covenant for alterations to a property in Sloane Street, and a discharge in favour of a policyholder of a mortgage on a freehold property in Kent. Authority to seal share transfers is covered by the same resolution. Then comes a report on Stock Exchange transactions completed since the previous meeting: sales and purchases, stocks acquired as the result of underwriting, and also contingent liabilities in connection with forthcoming issues we have underwritten, that is to say, shares we have agreed to buy in return for a small commission if the issue partly or wholly fails to attract the investing public.

And now we turn to new investments, first considering a few offers which brokers have made to our Managers during the previous twenty-four hours. Then we discuss some aspect of policy: for example, whether to exchange medium-dated Government stocks for others of longer date, or to invest in certain companies engaged in a new scientific development, or to reduce our holdings in, say, copper shares. A director who has lately been in Rhodesia gives us some first-hand views on the management of a certain mine and its attitude towards native labour. Its enlightened policy is reflected in output, but events in South Africa are having repercussions which we cannot ignore. Here, of course, there is room for different opinions, which are voiced by other directors—it happens that three members of the Board have visited Africa in the short space of six months. On such wider topics, the Board is usually briefed in advance by one of the Managers, whom I shall call Mr Wiseman, and he now joins the meeting to discuss his memorandum, in this case on the outlook for gilt-edged stocks.

'You suggest, Mr Wiseman, that these stocks are overpriced just now. Will you please give the Board further details?'

'Yes, Mr Chairman. The prices of British Government stocks have been rising fairly steadily since the end of November. The extent of the rise is indicated by the price of Consols $2\frac{1}{2}$ which has risen 8 per cent in six weeks from $50\frac{1}{4}$ to $54\frac{3}{8}$. Yet there doesn't seem to be any basic reason for the gilt-edged market to rise at this time. It may be due to Government support: this is the tax-gathering season when the Treasury has regular cash surpluses. Moreover, in November and December the Exchange Fund sold some millions of gold and foreign exchange for sterling, so that the Treasury is, for the time being, well supplied with the means of supporting the market. It seems more likely that the Treasury is buying in short-dated debt, including Treasury Bills, and that the Clearing Banks, already excessively liquid, are once again buying Government securities with redemption between five and fifteen years.'

At this point a director remarks that another reason for the rise is the possibility of a reduction in Bank Rate, which at the date of the meeting I am describing was being advocated in certain quarters. If this occurred, it would be regarded as an official indication that the crisis was over, and all markets would be likely to advance in price. The present buying might be in anticipation of such a move. Another director asks whether our Manager has taken account of the tonic effect of the Chancellor of the Exchequer's speech a day or two before to the American Chamber of Commerce, and in reply Mr Wiseman submits that this is a temporary factor.

Evidently this is not the moment to add to our gilt-edged investments, so I suggest to the Board that we put our current balance on deposit, and take another look at the situation at our next meeting. This is unanimously agreed.

The Board moves on to the 'State of Business' and we review the figures of the assurance policies written since the previous meeting. It is encouraging to note that the steady advance of recent months is being maintained and improved upon, in spite of changes in the Government's financial policy. The Agency Manager explains that the new pension facilities available to self-employed persons are adding substantially to our premium income. The Actuary reminds the Board that the tax will affect annuity business in a different way from normal life business, a factor which will make the current yield from an investment of more importance as applied to this section of our funds than the 'redemption' yield, i.e. the return which takes account not only of the interest but of the capital improvement between the price of the stock at the date of purchase and the date when the stock will become redeemable.

We now turn to property investments, and hear a report on the general progress of the past six months. We learn that more mortgages of substantial amounts have been completed than in recent years, due, no doubt, to an easing of restrictions, and in cases where Treasury consent has been required it appears to have been obtained without difficulty. Rather unusually, two substantial purchases totalling nearly £300,000 failed to reach completion at about the same time. In one case the proposed vendor withdrew at the last moment, and in the other our solicitor, fortified by the opinion of Counsel, had advised that the title offered was not satisfactory—a rare occurrence. House purchase schemes arranged with a large industrial firm and with a professional association had not so far resulted in much additional business, but more was to be expected in the spring.

The Board now adjourns for lunch, when we continue

talking a certain amount of 'shop' bearing on the adventurous business of the City, but also the political situation, the Test Match and the weather!

* * * * *

The reader is aware that my particular Board is composed of part-time directors (apart from the managing director) who come to the office for a weekly meeting but do not work in the business. Many City firms of course employ executive directors, and some Boards include both full-time and part-time members; but those of banks and insurance companies are usually on the latter basis. Week by week they help those of us who work in the same office every day to see the wood for the trees, and their wide experience and views are of great assistance to the various companies they serve. Not being beholden to one firm only for their bread and butter, part-time directors are able to speak their minds freely on the conduct of the business by its full-time executives and they provide an impartial check on proposals for development and expense which would not otherwise be available. Nothing is harder when engaged in the daily round of a business than to judge whether the right policy is being pursued at any time.

In my early days in the chair, I had the advantage of being able to talk things over with my father, who remained on the Board until his death in 1954. During five years he continued to take a keen but unobtrusive interest in all the affairs of the Institution, and although he could be very critical beforehand of some step I proposed to take, in the Board room he never failed to support the new Chairman. I suspect that criticism was sometimes designed to ensure that all sides of the question had been fully considered.

Among other services, part-time directors are often able to advise on current issues before the stage of formal negotiations is reached. Again, they can make helpful enquiries through channels which may not be directly available to the executive, for example, where questions of status are involved. But perhaps the most valuable asset of an efficient Board is the sense of unity and friendship which grows up among men of varied experience who meet together regularly with a common purpose.

4

Feeling our Way

The City of London is so steeped in history that, working there, one is constantly reminded that the problems which face us today are not very different from those which confronted Englishmen centuries ago. 'The cost of living', said a Londoner, 'makes it impossible for a good and upright man to live comfortably. It is difficult to afford one's children's education and all but impossible to bring them up safe from corruption.' These were not the only modern sentiments in a passage written in 1619, which suggests that we are still feeling our way.

Quite soon after taking up my appointment in Gracechurch Street, I addressed the Head Office staff on the policy of the Board, afterwards sending a printed copy of what I had said to every branch employee. Views differ on the value of such talks, which are frankly an effort and must not be overdone. Once introduced they must be kept up, but after ten years' experience I am convinced that there is no substitute for a full and regular disclosure of aims and methods by a business to its staff. If it can be shown quite simply why the work of every individual really matters a conscious sense of unity and purpose quickly develops. As most people are shy of talking in public, a two-way traffic in views and ideas must be encouraged through a staff magazine and a suggestions box; and before our larger meetings there is usually a less formal talk with executives and heads of departments.

In sharing ideas it is important that a Chairman should have a specific theme, and obviously announcements of an increase in wages and salaries will always be popular. But to suggest that pay is the only (or even the chief) topic of interest is to ignore other factors which make for good work and contentment, and some of the most satisfying meetings are those at which wider issues affecting the position and prospects of the company are discussed. Personally, I do not hesitate to mention the political situation when this seems called for, the City being, of course, particularly sensitive to public policy, and this practice is encouraged by the views of a former President of the Trades Union Congress, Sir Tom O'Brien, M.P., which appeared a few years ago in the National Provincial Bank *Review*. What he said on trade unions and national prosperity is equally appropriate to every type of worker, and particularly to those in the City who are in daily touch with international trade and finance. Sir Tom pointed out that 'there is a lot of wishful thinking about full employment. Too many people do not trouble to realize that it can continue only if ordinary folk living in many other countries are able and willing to buy our goods. . . . Once people don't want what we have to sell, or cannot buy our wares because they are too dear for their purses, then we've had it.' With equal cogency he asked how many people ever stopped to think that an end could come to the free markets of the world? 'Charts and curves are all very well for the economists and the statisticians. Ordinary people want things explained to them simply.'

The value of keeping employees fully in the picture has

been proved up to the hilt by Imperial Chemical Industries. It is no doubt easier to do this with a staff of two or three hundred than on a larger scale, yet this very large organization employing nearly 150,000 people uses similar techniques and has developed them to great advantage. Their system has little in common with the crude stopwatch idea formerly associated with 'work study', and during an 'Open Day' to which I was invited not long ago I was fascinated to see what amounts to an entirely new attitude to work put into action. I was of course already aware of the remarkable increase in output brought about by financial incentive schemes, but learned that the main benefits come from the analytical and critical thinking which work study evokes and a broader approach to all the company's affairs. Listening to the speakers, who included a factory manager, it was soon apparent that much more than a formula is being aimed at and applied. In studying work in the widest sense to improve efficiency, the goodwill is enlisted of every employee in office as well as factory, and it is shown that basically 'every individual is the manager of his own job'. Side by side with better earnings, the record of absenteeism and accidents has gone down as the men gain confidence and their interest in the job increases.

In their drive to improve productivity, ICI are enjoying the keen cooperation of the trade unions, and I was told that trade unionists are often more receptive to new ideas and techniques than some of those at managerial level. We are all apt to rely on experience but are not always ready to learn from it. New ideas are constantly up against inertia, which can be a considerable obstacle in large firms, and this is just as true of business organizations in the City of London as in industry.

As I am attempting to give a picture of a particular business in the City and how it is run, this chapter will comprise a few passages from talks given to the staff of the United Kingdom Provident Institution. The effect of timing is very important, for by linking the affairs of a business with the news of the moment a sense of urgency and heightened interest can be created. Thus in talking on the cost of living, on September 20, 1951, I said that on the previous morning the Board had held its usual Wednesday meeting at 12.15, and had taken certain decisions of considerable importance to the staff. On the same evening at 9.15 the Prime Minister had announced that a General Election would be held next month. There was, clearly, no direct connection between these two happenings, but in practice the Board's decisions were related to the wider economic background, which would be affected to a considerable degree by the results of the forthcoming poll. Yet whatever the colour of the new Parliament might be, the high cost of living was likely to persist for some time to come. It was partly the effect of excessive Government expenditure—a problem which all parties should face. It was also due to the high cost of imported materials, especially from the dollar area, which in turn was related to rearmament and the war in Korea.

'For some time', I explained, 'the Board has been fully aware of the problem which the high cost of living presents to the staff. The directors are equally concerned about the rising costs of conducting this business. Life assurance is highly competitive, and is based on long-term contracts at premium rates which are fixed for ten, fifteen or twenty years. Unlike a manufacturer, who can usually revise his prices in the course of a contract if costs increase, the underwriter has no such safeguard. While our business is well up on 1938, the costs of procuring it have risen still more, and the task of the Actuaries in meeting all our obligations is increasingly severe. We can, of course, afford to take a long-term view, but it is clear that the Board must be very careful in adding to our costs, especially if the present inflation persists.'

The salaries of the permanent staff carried substantial pensions. The Head Office scale had been revised in 1947 and also in 1950; it was too soon for the Board to alter the scale again, with its further pension liabilities, but we had been exploring ways and means of assisting the staff in a period of fluctuating costs without adding to our permanent commitments.

'Happily, as I think, we have found a flexible means for helping to meet present conditions in the form of the bonus. At present this is payable to the indoor staffs at the branches annually and at Head Office triennially, but the Board has decided instead to pay these staffs an annual bonus on an increased scale during the present triennium and to extend the same principle to the outside staff. In addition, a special grant will be made to married men with two or more children under sixteen. . . . When addressing you on an earlier occasion I suggested that to meet rising costs two people might have to do the work of three if the staff is to be adequately paid, and this is still truer today. It does not mean that persons will be discharged, but it does mean that additions to the staff both at Head Office and branches will be made with great caution, and that every department should aim at getting the most out of its existing personnel. The question of lengthening office hours was considered, but instead of taking this step we propose to ask for up to two hours per week of unpaid overtime whenever the state of the departmental work requires.'

Referring again to the economic problems facing the country and the insurance business, I said these would be affected by the result of the General Election, but not perhaps to the extent which would be suggested from opposing platforms in the next few weeks. It was well to preserve a sense of perspective, especially in the affairs of an Institution which had successfully ridden the storms of more than a century.

'The habit of running ourselves down is a well-known British failing, which is apt to be seen at its worst during election campaigns. I am therefore going to conclude with a quotation from Lord Hankey's recent Romanes Lecture at Oxford. He has served Governments of all political colours during half a century and now sits on the cross-benches of the House of Lords.

> "It is my unalterable conviction," Lord Hankey said, "that the steady, unassuming folk far exceed in number the malcontents, idlers, slackers, lightning strikers, and so forth, and that at bottom we are still the same solid, kindly, good-tempered and fundamentally God-fearing people as of yore, rather easy-going, but absolutely reliable in emergency."

'I am sure that the staff will join with the Board in facing the future with the same determination to carry on the best traditions of our Institution, whatever the weather ahead.'

* * * * *

The year 1952 saw new achievements in many British industries, and the record figures of the insurance business were no exception. Using this as my theme early in January 1953, I reminded the staff that in the previous April I had referred to the sterling-dollar gap and to the alarming fall then taking place in the gold reserves. By increasing exports, decreasing imports and adopting certain monetary measures, the Government had now nearly stopped the outflow of gold. Britain's credit stood very much higher, and that helped our trading position and standard of living. In the aircraft industry, we were leading the world, and orders worth many millions of pounds were being executed for overseas buyers. Shipbuilders had work in hand worth £670 million, much of this huge figure being in foreign currency. British engineering firms had secured contracts in Canada, the United States and New Zealand in face of keen competition, and steel output in 1952 was an all-time record.

'While we can feel a just pride in these achievements,' I said, 'the financial position of industry as a whole presents a grave problem, which insurance can help to solve. I refer to the shortage of savings. Some of you may have read an article by Mr S. P. Chambers, a deputy chairman of Imperial Chemical Industries, on "Industry at the Cross Roads", which recently appeared in their staff magazine. He showed in the simplest terms that the country is not saving enough to increase the amount of capital which is behind the workers in the form of machines and equipment; and that a big cut in Government expenditure is essential if our standards of living are to be maintained. "There is one exception to the general rule that no savings are taking place," Mr Chambers writes. "Some saving is in fact taking place through the medium of insurance companies and pension funds to the extent of over £200 million per annum." Yet he goes on to describe this as a mere fraction of what is needed by industry to maintain and replace machinery, let alone improve it, and to replace stocks of materials. The Americans are saving ten times as much per worker as we are—no wonder their productivity is higher. In terms of life assurance it boils down to this: the more policies we sell, the more the saving and the better for the country.

'Economists are fond of talking about the money incentive, but may I end by reminding you that this is by no means our only motive? In a recent talk at a British Institute of Management Conference, Lord Verulam rightly said there are at least three others: there is the sense of achievement, of getting something done; the sense of companionship ("bitterly missed the moment it is lost"); and the sense of trusteeship ("working to see that what is passed on is better than when we got it"). It is helpful for us to be aware of these factors, because results are not so obvious when we work at a desk as to the man who works in a carpenter's shop. I believe that all these incentives are evident in our Institution and will be an increasing source of strength in the future.'

★ ★ ★ ★ ★

A well-known psychologist has doubts whether there is such a thing as a normal person—the other fellow is always peculiar! Whether or not that is so, there are certainly no normal times today, assuming there ever were. With this opening for a talk in December, 1955, I reminded the staff that in the last six years we had faced a devaluation of the £, two General Elections, the war in Korea and the cold war elsewhere, further inflation, a round of strikes, and finally the Credit Squeeze. All the time we have had to fix rates of premium for many years ahead. I had always emphasized the view that new business and the prosperity of the staff go hand in hand. Inflation was a big subject on which the experts differed. Some say that too much capital expenditure is the basic cause, others blame excessive wages in trades where output has not risen to match wages. But increased pay need not be inflationary provided it came out of higher output. This was the message of the British Productivity Council, and I had invited our branch managers in certain areas to cooperate with the Council in furthering this important campaign.

'In recent years,' I said, 'we have avoided relating the Institution's salaries strictly to the Cost of Living Index, which is designed for industrial rather than office workers, and the pensions which come into our rewards are not yet extended to all workers. The cost of living is, of course, no new problem. In a book I am reading on the reign of Charles I,[1] it is given as a reason for emigrating to America by a lawyer with a good practice in London. [Here I quoted the passage already quoted on page 49). That was in the year 1619. Even so, the cost of living still has a bearing on the levels of pay, and between February, 1954, when our salary scales were last revised and the autumn Budget this year, the official index rose by 10 points, partly offset by reductions in income tax and increased personal allowances. In view of the substantial rise in our output represented by increased new business, the Board has now agreed to increase salaries by 12½ per cent, and to raise the maximum of each grade of the Head Office scale.'

In a further reference to output, I stressed the value of our Suggestions Scheme, and mentioned for the benefit of newcomers that entries are judged by the Secretary and a com-

[1] *Charles I and the Puritan Upheaval* by Allen French (George Allen & Unwin).

mittee of officials which can award a prize for 'any worth-while suggestion showing originality, interest in ones own job and the work of the office generally, assisting the new business effort and promoting the good name of the Institution'. No names are disclosed in the first case: any ideas put into the suggestions box are typed and numbered before they are judged purely on their merits.

'I am pleased to announce two further awards this morning. One will go to our chief clerk at Watford for an improved memorandum form which should reduce printing costs, save filing space, and reduce the weight of mail from Head Office to branches and *vice versa*, an important item now that postal rates have been raised. The other award will go to a member of the correspondence department, who suggests that every branch should clearly type the full name and postal address of the proposer and attach this to the proposal form, as quite a lot of time is wasted at Head Office in trying to decipher the proposer's handwriting. Welsh addresses in particular are apt to cause headaches! This is one of those very simple ideas but no less valuable on that account.'

I concluded this particular talk by quoting another passage from the book on the reign of Charles I which might have been written of the City at almost any time since the Second World War. 'In describing the citizens of London of the early 1600s, with its "one bridge but many ferries, its few theatres but many taverns, its new public coaches, its half-timbered houses overhanging narrow and miry streets," Mr Allen French adds:

' "Picturesque though they are to us, and often amusing, these English were the moderns of their day, earning their livings, solving their own problems, working their way from decision to decision, from year to year. . . . Much was puzzling and very much was new. From old formulas, applied to current conditions, they were developing fresh principles . . . they were men and women under trial, seeking to understand and to decide."

'All of us, I suggest, whatever our position in the City today, are like those burgesses of 300 years ago—we are still exploring fresh ground, we are still seeking to understand and to decide. Unlike Mr Allen French, some foreigners who don't understand our outlook and temperament think that we "muddle through"—perhaps we do. On the other hand it may be that our gift for give and take, and for agreeing to differ, is actually our greatest asset, explaining why in political stability we still lead the world.'

II

MONEY AT WORK

5

A Useful Commodity

Seventeen clerks and two doorkeepers, 'furnished with ink, paper and sand', made up the staff and equipment of the Bank of England in 1694, when William III granted a charter to form the bank to some merchants who lent him £12,000,000 to pay for the war against France. Today, the Bank employs six thousand people and its premises cover three and a half acres.

As the central source of our currency, the Bank of England prints notes and treasury bills, and at the Royal Mint on Tower Hill five hundred million metal coins are produced every year. A large proportion of these are made for Commonwealth and foreign governments. Yet money is not something to be manufactured without reference to exact standards. If this happens, and the printing presses are set going as they were in Germany and Austria after both the world wars, money quickly ceases to have any value. Millions of marks were then needed to pay for a bus ticket; I recall that when my father launched *The European Commercial* in 1920 to help in reviving international trade, he had a suite of rooms at the best hotel in Vienna for less than £5 a week.

The first bankers were goldsmiths, whose receipts for the safe deposit of gold and silver coins and plate were gradually used and accepted as currency. As international trade developed, the units of money in various countries were related to the value of gold, and the Gold Standard came into being. In the original sense of the term this has gone by the board, but the 'exact standards' I have already mentioned still take account of gold and in various ways the value of our currency is controlled by the Government. Moreover, a jury of the Worshipful Company of Goldsmiths has tested coins every March since 1248, and the results are reported in the following May to the King's Remembrancer, in the presence of the Chancellor of the Exchequer. The Bank of England in conjunction with the Treasury issues notes to the joint stock banks, which in turn issue them to the public.

The Bank is the scene of a colourful ceremony every evening, when a detachment of the Brigade of Guards enters its gates to protect the establishment overnight. In 1780, at the time of the Gordon Riots, the mob attacked the Bank of England after destroying Newgate Prison. Horse and foot guards were summoned to its defence. Since then, the troops have marched every evening from Westminster to the City to take up their post at sunset. As Dickens relates in *Barnaby Rudge*, the whole of the City was under arms during the Gordon Riots. The staff of Hoare's Bank in Fleet Street were issued with muskets, some of which still hang on the walls of that bank today.

Both the history and practice of banking serve to underline that money is first and foremost a commodity. Although it is only useful when exchanged for other commodities and services and much of it is now made of paper, money is not something which exists only on paper. Hence more money in the pay packet or on the dividend warrant, unless matched by a higher output of the goods it will buy, may simply result in higher prices and cause further inflation. Although bank money and credit and the use of cheques now play a far larger part in the business affairs of the nation than coins and notes, and the rate at which money circulates is another very important consideration, this does not alter the fact that money is a commodity and that its value bears a definite relation to supply. This brings me again to my own business, for money is the raw material of life assurance. Whether writing policies or paying claims we deal in money, every day we are putting money to work, and no trade in the City is more alive to the vital importance of a sound currency and of the need to bring this home to the man in the street.

★ ★ ★ ★ ★

The ways in which the City of London puts money to work are many. Insurance companies use it in several ways and the American offices have coined the term 'double duty' money to describe the funds they hold. In the first place, the premiums paid by the policyholder are lent to the Government, to industry and to individuals, so paying for plant and equipment and other assets which in their turn add to the wealth of the community. Secondly, as the money is paid back to the policyholder (or his dependents) when his insurance matures, it does further duty by providing for his personal needs, whether these be for a house or a car or a school bill or to finance his retirement.

The greater part of the money entrusted to insurance companies is invested through the Stock Exchange, but a substantial proportion is lent direct to policyholders. An insurance company will usually grant a loan of an amount up to 90 per cent of the surrender value of the policy, although the more normal method is for the borrower to deposit the policy as security against an advance from a bank, which in granting credit will also take account of the borrower's local standing. Another method of financing a new project is through an advance on the strength of existing assets coupled with an endowment policy, which increases in value from year to year until, on maturity, it pays off the loan. Where large sums are involved, policies may be taken out on the lives of several senior executives in the business concerned.

Not many people would associate the City of London with greenhouses in the Channel Islands, yet in practice life assurance policies are playing a useful part in tomato growing, which is a staple industry there. Several of our policy-holders have obtained bank advances to enable them to enter the industry on their own account and to purchase small plots of land on which to build greenhouses. One of these has now extended the original area of glass over three times. Tomato growing is an all-the-year-round business and as soon as one annual crop is finished preparations go ahead for the next, involving a continual outlay for labour, new plants, manures and heating. All this expense is incurred out of season when no income is being received, and it is then that our money is at work, helping to provide temporary finance until the income from the new year's crop is available.

Another example of the same kind, this time in Sussex, concerns a firm of poultry and egg packers now employing a staff of sixty. Shortly after the war the proprietor died, leaving his wife and son (just out of the Forces) to carry on the business. On the advice of their bank manager the widow took out a life policy to provide money in the event of her death so that the business might be kept going. The son also has taken out policies. The firm has since progressed rapidly, and over half a million eggs now pass through its hands every week.

Money provided by an insurance company has recently enabled a firm of provincial outfitters to enlarge its premises. A substantial mortgage helped them to buy the freehold of a building which adjoined their two shops, and all are now merged in one block. Our assistance has not only allowed the proprietors to keep control of the firm in the family's hands but has provided them with one of the most valuable sites in the town.

At the end of the war a Scottish policyholder decided that he would build and operate his own textile mill. After forcing his way through the many controls which at that time hampered developments of this kind, he found himself faced with the problem of finance. His factory was built and in production, but most of his resources had been used in getting the business under way. To obtain the benefits of full output more cash was needed for additional machinery and raw materials. He had a long connection with our Institution and this, together with his obvious personal qualities of initiative and enthusiasm, encouraged us to lend him the necessary money. From the way the business has prospered and increased each year our confidence has been fully justified. I had to use some persuasion to get this particular mortgage approved by the Board, and it gave me great satisfaction to see how the mill had prospered when I visited it some years later.

Money provided by the City is also at work in the theatre. Some twenty years ago a young screen actor just reaching star status was introduced to us by one of our brokers. Since that time his life policy has been used as security for bank loans to purchase a house, to educate his children and to tide him over occasional long periods of resting. When he reaches the age at which he will be classed as a 'veteran', the policy will mature and will provide this now distinguished actor with a regular income to supplement his reduced earnings. Another personal success story comes from a country solicitor who now has a thriving practice. As a young law clerk he took out an endowment with-profit policy. Some years later he decided to try to qualify, and in due course had to take time off to prepare for the final examination. This involved loss of pay; as he was by then married, it was a bold decision to make; but with the help of loans on his policies and other savings he was able to carry on his studies—and duly passed his finals.

Lastly I may mention the dollar export drive. A policy-holder who has long been in business as a horticulturist decided a few years ago to export dry bulbs to Canada, the United States and South Africa. His insurances helped him to secure the finance needed to launch this new project. Although this part of the business started in a small way it has increased year by year, and he reports that these dollar exports are now being developed in a very satisfactory way.

All these examples of money lent direct to a person or firm, whether by a bank or insurance company, are easy to grasp. Money that is put to work through the Stock Exchange is not such plain sailing, since a good deal goes into existing stocks and shares, and does not directly add to the volume of investments. For that reason the question is sometimes asked whether insurance institutions do, in fact, contribute as much to the nation's investments as they claim. We are also criticized for being too cautious in our attitude to risk capital, that is to say, money required for new or developing ventures. At the same time, by a curious contradiction, the insurance companies are alleged to have too much of a hold on industry and even to wish to control it.

In reply to the argument that purchases of existing Ordinary stocks, as distinct from new issues, do not benefit industry but merely represent a change of ownership, the Government loans issued during the war afford an analogy. The loans were a channel for savings for the war effort. The man who invested in some existing Government security was contributing just as much as the man who bought the new National War Bonds. Moreover, all purchases of industrial securities tend to sustain share prices, and improve the receptivity of the market, while sellers of existing shares often reinvest the proceeds in new issues. In a recent speech I emphasized the importance of such investments and said that a policyholder is not only protecting himself and his family when he pays his yearly premium but is also helping the nation in a positive way.

'As an example, through our investment in the Manchester Ship Canal Company, the members of the Institution have helped to build the new Queen Elizabeth II dock, the largest oil dock in Great Britain. How 600 men toiled day and night for three years in all weathers to construct this dock is a saga of modern Elizabethan enterprise which deserves the widest publicity. In all such developments the institutional investor will continue to play an indispensable role.'

The suggestion that we wish to control industry through our investments probably arises from the size of our operations. Size in business tends to arouse suspicion, which may be a healthy factor, since Englishmen like variety and doing things for themselves, and the scope for personal initiative is often in inverse ratio to size. Yet with life assurance, when the change in the price level is taken into account, the amount of business written today does not show much increase on 1938, and the sum of insurance resources is still small in relation to the value of all the securities quoted on the Stock Exchange.

* * * * *

Many people think of the Stock Exchange as a sort of casino, and of course there are speculators in Throgmorton Street, although their role is not very significant in relation to the total business transacted. But taking risks in putting money to work plays an important role in the City of London, and without this necessary and adventurous factor a great amount of economic activity would not take place. Every time an investor lends money to a new firm or an established concern to finance a fresh invention or development, he is taking a risk. If the venture fails, his money is lost; if it succeeds, he gets the reward of his enterprise. The border-line between risk taking and speculation in the disreputable sense of the word is a fine one—if a venture succeeds it is usually regarded as shrewd business, if it fails it is condemned as gambling! The alternative to this method of risking money would involve some form of State compulsion, and the economic test would tend to go by the board. Moreover, the losses would be borne by the public at large.

Tony Weller aptly described stocks and shares as 'things that go up and down in the City', and they are, of course, merely pieces of paper issued in return for sums of money which are spent, for example, in starting a shop or building a factory. In return for this money, with which the borrower has equipped his business, part of any profits earned are repaid to the lender or shareholder as interest or dividend. Thanks to the Stock Exchange—and I refer to the exchanges in other cities in Britain as well as in London—an owner of shares can nearly always sell them and get his money back, or some of it if the business in which he has invested has not proved successful. The Stock Exchange is thus, first and foremost, a convenient market through which people can lend their savings and realize them later with the minimum of trouble. The fact that there is also a professional trade in stocks and shares, by persons and firms whose business it is to make a living out of buying and selling them, also helps industry. Good shares normally reflect good management, shares which lose their value reflect bad management, so the stock market tends to be a barometer of efficiency and to keep business up to the mark. This barometer is valuable in another way. It sets a price on money for different types of trade and industry. Hence when a firm needs to raise more money it can invite the public to subscribe for its shares on a basis which can be exactly measured. Rates of interest are normally a measure of risk. If the money is wanted for a highly speculative enterprise which may well fail, the borrowers will obviously have to pay a high rate of interest or dividend to their shareholders. A safe venture, on the other hand, can be financed on more moderate terms. I must mention here that the rate of interest means little or nothing unless related to the current value of a share: for example, a dividend of 20 per cent on a share nominally worth £1 but which, due to good management and value of the assets it represents, is now priced at £4, is actually a 5 per cent dividend.

Although securities are bought and sold under strict safeguards for the protection of investors, the Stock Exchange does not fix the prices; they are determined by the laws of supply and demand in this free and active market. About ten thousand securities are officially quoted and their total value is more than £35,000 million, British Government securities accounting for nearly half of this total. It is estimated that four-fifths of all Britain's industry and commerce is carried on by companies with quoted capital. Some other figures recently issued by the Council of the Stock Exchange show that nine out of ten shareholdings in industrial companies are of less than £500.

No City institution has been more vigorous in recent years in making itself known, and in 1953 the Stock Exchange opened a public gallery to enable visitors to watch its business taking place. A leaflet handed to the visitor gives such an excellent account of the Stock Exchange and its work that the rest of this chapter is taken almost word for word from it.

It is pointed out that in the heart of the City of London the visitor is watching one of the great financial markets of the world. In this active, competitive market, securities of all kinds are freely and fairly bought and sold—Government loans and the shares of thousands of commercial and industrial companies. Here is transacted business that comes not only from all over Britain but from every continent. He is looking down at the floor of the 'House'—the name by which Members know the Stock Exchange. The floor covers about three-quarters of an acre. The oldest part of the present building dates from 1820, but the Stock Exchange, as an institution, is much older. It was in the seventeenth century that the Government, and a number of trading enterprises, began to raise money by public subscription, and stocks and shares were issued. Towards the end of the seventeenth century the early stockbrokers used to meet in the old Royal Exchange and later carried on their business in the coffee houses round Change Alley. It was not until 1773 that a meeting of stockbrokers decided that they needed a house of their own: they took over a building at the corner of Threadneedle Street and Sweetings Alley, and from this has grown, step by step with the expansion of British industry and commerce, the great financial market we know today.

The spectator is further informed that the men he sees in groups, or moving about, are Members and their clerks. Generally some 2,500 are on the floor of the House, but many others are at work in their offices and in maintaining contact with their clients. There are two types of member—brokers and jobbers. Jobbers are themselves dealers in stocks and shares; they do not deal with the public but only with other members, i.e. the brokers, who have quite a different function. Brokers act as agents for investors, who instruct them to buy or sell securities; it is their business to carry out these instructions to the best advantage of their clients, and for this they receive a fixed rate of commission on each sale or purchase.

The scene viewed from the gallery may appear confusing. In fact, the informal groups of members represent different 'markets', which by long tradition occupy their own position on the floor. Each market deals in one group of securities—Government stocks, industrial shares, oil shares, mining shares, etc. Against a pillar or wall near his 'pitch' a jobber may hang a price list of the stocks in which he specializes. Some prices are marked in blue, indicating a rise, and others in red, showing a fall. Deals are recorded only in the notebooks of the jobber and broker. No more formal bargain is made even for the largest transactions, which as I mentioned in my first chapter are carried out by word of mouth.

The men with blue buttons in their lapels are the clerks of the jobbers and brokers, and in a working day they may walk as much as eight miles! The attendants in blue and red uniforms and gold-braided top hats are the Stock Exchange 'waiters' named after their coffee-house predecessors. From eleven stands placed about the floor of the House, waiters control much of the internal communications system, which includes large boards with illuminated figures. These have no reference to shares or prices: they are to call members to receive messages. Other boards summon members to answer calls on the private telephone system, each firm having its own number.

More exciting for City men can be the four Bank Rate indicators or lighted signs. Every Thursday at 11.45 a.m. the Government broker arrives from the Bank of England bringing news of any change in the Bank Rate. A similar board shows the Bank Rates prevailing in New York, Paris Brussels and Amsterdam. Important company news is notified to members by messages flashed on the three 'Translux' screens, but in contrast to these modern methods, each waiter's stand is equipped with speaking-tubes through which he can give messages to different parts of the building.

From time to time shouting may be heard above the general hubbub. It may be a waiter—many have the voices of sergeant-majors—seeking some member for whom he has a message, but occasionally a jobber may raise his voice to offer or bid for the shares in which he deals. A visitor who is in the gallery at 2.15 p.m. may hear the sound of loud rattles, an old-fashioned but curiously effective signal. This means that no more transactions can be recorded on the day's list, from which the share prices published in the newspapers next day are compiled. Rattles are sounded again at 3.15 to tell members that they may smoke during the last quarter of an hour of business, and fifteen minutes later the closing of the House is announced by a third rattle signal. But this is not the end of the working day, as dealings continue on the telephone, often up to a late hour, in the offices of brokers and jobbers. There is always correspondence to deal with, and of course the study of industrial and financial reports is never-ending.

The number of bargains marked during the day may total as many as 15,000, and in the price lists which later appear in the Press the number of transactions in each 'market' is shown in brackets. So behind each of the figures which may fill two pages of our morning newspaper lies a story of business enterprise which has often sprung from the small personal savings which are providing much of the working capital of British industry today.

6

How We Invest It

I am often asked why a City chairman so seldom commits himself to more than moderate optimism in his speech at the annual general meeting when dealing with what he invariably describes as 'the outlook'. The answer (or part of it) is that the impact of events outside the control of those who look after other people's money is greater than those who entrust it to us usually appreciate. Quite normal events and occasions, and not only crises, may quickly affect investments, and, indeed, one of the advantages an insurance institution can offer its clients is peace of mind, by relieving them of the anxiety which the care of money is apt to involve.

In looking through some records of our annual meetings a century ago I came across a reference in the chairman's speech of 1852 which illustrates my point. Our business had been adversely affected in 1851, Robert Warner said, because the Great Exhibition had 'unusually diverted the attention of all classes from the ordinary course of business'. Happily, a hundred years later, the Festival of Britain had no such repercussions; on the contrary 1951 brought us excellent results. Even local situations can have quick reactions: during the London bus strike in 1958 some of the City's business was slowed down, not on account of transport difficulties in our 'square mile' but due to concern and discussions which took our minds off the job, and in total, consumed a lot of valuable time.

Our particular company was founded in the restive era that followed the Reform Bill, and anyone who supposes that economic ups and downs are a new feature will find interesting parallels in the age of Peel and Cobden. Yet making every allowance for the difficulties which confront business in every period, I cannot think that a Victorian Board of directors faced so many problems in putting money to work as we have had to meet of late years. A City firm which recently celebrated its coming of age had opened its doors in July 1937, when Bank Rate was 2 per cent and income tax 5s 0d. By 1941 income tax had doubled, and when the war ended a series of drastic changes began. These were listed in a brochure published to celebrate the firm's anniversary, and in what follows I shall not alter the rather salty references to nationalization, understandable on the part of brokers whose range of business was thereby curtailed:

1946 Shortages and 'Daltons'. Coal nationalized.
1947 Fuel crisis. India given to Nehru.
1948 Railways and electricity grabbed. 2% Stamp Duty.
1949 Gas goes out. Sterling devalued.
1950 Second Labour Government. Korean War.
1951 Steel snatch. Gold reserves crisis. Conservative Government. Bank Rate 2½%. Funding operation.
1952 Bank Rate raised to 4%.
1953 Exit Truman, Stalin. Steel denationalized. Bank Rate 3½%.
1954 End of Excess Profits Levy. Bank Rate down to 3%.

1955 Bank Rate $3\frac{1}{2}$% then $4\frac{1}{2}$%. Strikes. Income Tax 8/6d. Industrial shares index hits high. Autumn Budget. Sir Winston Churchill retires. Enter Bulganin and Khrushchev.

1956 Bank Rate $5\frac{1}{2}$%. Suez crisis and Hungarian Revolution.

1957 Bank Rate raised from 5% to 7%. Government Securities index at new low. Sputnik new high.

1958 Bank Rate Tribunal report. Birth of Zeta. Bank Rate reduced to 6%.

The importance attached by the City to Bank Rate is due, of course, to its repercussions on other interest rates. As its name implies, this is the rate at which the Bank of England makes loans to the Discount Market. Most variable rates of interest in this country, for example those which the banks charge for overdrafts or pay on deposits, are geared to Bank Rate, and all this explains the excitement in the City whenever Bank Rate is changed.

The significance of interest rates generally is brought out by an analysis of my own Institution's investments over the past fifty years which provides an interesting commentary on this aspect of financial history. In 1900 we did not hold any Government stocks and as late as 1910 only a negligible amount. Until 1914, Consols yielding 3 per cent must have seemed very unattractive, but during the First World War the Government issued redeemable stocks (i.e. those which will be paid off at their full face value at a fixed date or dates) in great quantities, and patriotism combined with higher interest rates no doubt explained why this class of securities accounted for nearly half our total assets by 1923. Other notable features in this particular investment story are:

(1) The increase in Foreign Securities in 1910 and 1929 and their virtual disappearance today, except for American stocks.
(2) The increase in ordinary shares after 1930.
(3) The rise in property investments since 1932.
(4) The rise in Mortgages to a maximum of 18·4% on December 31, 1938.
(5) The fall in Ground Rents from 30% on December 31, 1905, to 11·7% on December 31, 1923.
(6) The amount of loans on policies which rose steadily to a maximum of £2,180,000 on December 31, 1932, but fell to £720,000 in 1950. There has since been some increase, but as these loans are made to policyholders usually as a matter of routine the amount cannot be forecast precisely when we are making our investment plans.

In looking at any list of investments which analyses the amounts of various stocks held on a percentage basis, it is important to realize that the rise or fall in values from time to time, and not only the purchases or sales of additional securities, affects the distribution. The value of any portfolio which contains ordinary shares has risen greatly in recent years. In 1930, when my company obtained powers to invest in ordinary shares, the economic balloon was pretty well deflated, but in 1956 it was again much inflated and prices are still very high in 1958.

* * * * *

Side by side with our English investments we now have large holdings of 'common shares', as ordinary shares are called across the Atlantic, and this dollar portfolio has taken me to Wall Street several times since the war. When discussing these investments I found it fascinating to discover that the ablest minds in Wall Street are still conscious of the 'Covered Wagon' in framing their plans. Sitting in air-conditioned offices, aided by every gadget that modern science can devise, it at first seems paradoxical that bankers and brokers should be talking as a matter of course of opportunities for further expansion not only in the West but in other areas. For example, in 1954 I was told that the United States Steel Corporation was putting up a new plant in New Jersey 'to improve its competitive position in the Eastern States'. The idea of such an industrial giant being still in the least bit concerned about competition was frankly an eye-opener. Similarly, it was news to learn that most market agreements between the oil companies had been torn up, so that the public was getting the benefit of full competition in supplies and prices. But the Covered Wagon was most in evidence in discussing the shares of public utility companies, banks and stores. 'Continuous growth ahead' was predicted for a power company in Delaware; on the other hand a similar undertaking in another State was said to have no such prospects, since it was operating in an area where conditions were highly regulated. While the shares of certain New York banks offered small growth prospects, greater appreciation was expected in the shares of banks in Cleveland, Ohio and Kansas City. Those in California were not favoured, as the tremendous expansion there had still to be digested.

Another factor in Wall Street is the increasing influence of the institutional investor who, as in the City of London, is providing a very substantial volume of new money for the stock market. Not only insurance companies and pension funds but also savings banks are now permitted to invest some of their funds in equities; incidentally insurance companies and banks are more rigorously controlled in America than they are in Britain. The growth of unit trusts, or 'mutual funds' as they are called over there, is also helping to sustain share prices, and all these developments are aided by skilful advertising. I watched a very effective television programme sponsored by the National City Bank of New York, a nightly '11 o'clock News' feature given by John F. Mackeffery. With dignity and humour he summarized the news of the day, with a suitable footnote on the merits of having an account with the National City Bank. Actual examples of help given by the bank to house purchasers, farmers, etc., are sometimes included in these broadcasts.

When again visiting America in 1958, I saw the new U.S. Steel works in New Jersey in full operation. Two giant plants for making steel and steel tubes had been built by 10,000 men working day and night for eighteen months. Like the adjoining Levittown, these plants were erected on farm land, and as most of the men working on the site owned cars, there were great traffic jams on the narrow country roads. Today, there are over forty miles of new wide roads in the works area, which covers about six square miles. The plants are named after Benjamin Fairless, a coal miner's son from Ohio who guided the U.S. Steel Corporation through seventeen of its most dramatic years, and are the most up to date of their kind in the country. Natural gas is piped from Texas to supply part of the fuel required.

About 6,000 men are employed, and many of them were new to the job when U.S. Steel moved into this district. To get the Corporation assimilated into the area was described as 'good public relations'. All employees are paid on an incentive basis, which takes quality as well as quantity into account, and large notices with this theme are displayed in both plants, e.g. 'Quality brings Business—more business, more work'; 'Our customers are our real Job Insurance'; 'Now, more than ever before, quality counts'. Watching miles of red-hot steel passing through rollers, nearly all handled by press buttons, I was glad to see that the finished rolls were labelled with a piece of blackboard chalk before being put into stock—a pleasant human touch in a robot world.

All this activity has its counterpart in Wall Street. I believe that some of those who work there drive themselves far too hard (and Americans say that it can be a very ruthless place), but this great energy in providing finance for new enterprise goes far to explain the economic prowess of America today. The pace of living, in Manhattan at any rate, may be partly ascribed to the climate, but I found myself vigorously defending our more leisurely *tempo* in a discussion with a friend who was critical of England on this score. By giving time to other interests, I suggested, we gain a sense of perspective which helps our daily work and enables us to escape the feverish pressure which business, at the other extreme, can so easily involve. But generalizations are dangerous, and this whole question was aptly summed up by a friend from Virginia who remarked to me that if the British would speed up a bit and the Americans slow down a bit, this would make an ideal combination. As the links between the City and Wall Street have been strengthened in recent years, and finance is now being provided on a joint basis for projects on both sides of the Atlantic and in many parts of the Commonwealth, there should be great scope for this ideal combination to prove itself in the years ahead.

* * * * *

To complete the picture I am trying to paint of how we invest our policyholders' money, I shall now describe what we term our 'blueprint'. This is the provisional plan drawn up at the beginning of each year for the disposal of the money which we expect to be available for investment in the coming twelve months, some of it from stocks and shares due to be redeemed, but mostly new money paid to us as premiums. The blueprint is drafted by our experts after a preliminary discussion with the chairman, and is then submitted to the Board for detailed consideration and approval. In making our forecasts for 1958 we considered that the economic climate in which investment decisions would be made would be dominated by three issues: the continued battle for reinforcing the position of sterling; the business situation in the United States; and the trend of world commodity prices with its impact on the purchasing power of the primary producing countries.

Sterling was then emerging from a difficult year with the reserves (excluding what has been borrowed in dollars and must soon be repaid) impaired, and one of the main tasks ahead would be to repair the damage and fortify the reserves. The recent changes at the Treasury had not altered the fundamental objectives of British economic policy, to fight inflation and stabilize the value of the pound, but one of the paradoxical results of Mr Thorneycroft's disappearance from the scene might be to prolong the era of a 7 per cent Bank Rate somewhat longer than would otherwise have occurred and to make the next Budget more austere.

The United States economy was another great imponderable. What the President had termed the 'breather' has sufficient momentum behind it to carry the level of industrial production (and probably of security prices) to still lower levels during the next few months, but there were powerful forces making for recovery, including consumer buying which was defying all talk of recession.

Finally, commodity prices had fallen to a level at which the purchasing power of the primary producing countries was seriously curtailed, but this might help the United Kingdom terms of trade and balance of payments. On the other hand it would induce certain members of the sterling area—among them Malaya, Rhodesia, Ghana—to draw down their balances and thus put more strain on sterling. A pick up in the American business situation would help the commodity markets, but there were signs of overproduction in copper, oil and tin, which, irrespective of changes across the Atlantic, were likely to make for a still lower level of prices.

Taking account of all these factors, we thought that 1958 would remain a year of relatively dear money, but with the trend moving towards lower interest rates. In making up our blueprint we therefore continued to put the main emphasis on investment in fixed-interest securities, with a tendency to favour those with reasonably long dates. We should probably look back on 1957-58 as a period of exceptionally high interest rates, so this was the time to secure those high rates for as long a period as possible. As the movement would be towards lower rates, since it was almost inconceivable that we should endure a 7 per cent Bank Rate until the end of the year, the purchase of gilt-edged securities should be concentrated as far as possible in the next few months. We further expected that for the general run of British industrial ordinary shares, 1958 was likely to prove a hazardous period. The effect of the credit squeeze on profits, and even more on distributions, would become increasingly apparent, and this should therefore offer opportunity for adding to our holdings of good equities.

As events turned out, we were able to adhere pretty closely to the foregoing plans, although equity prices remained at higher levels than had seemed likely when the blueprint was made. Nor did we foresee how quickly the measures to counter inflation would take effect, or how large the increase in the gold reserves would actually prove to be due to the heavy fall in the price of imported materials and the consequent improvement in what are called the terms of trade—an example of the world-wide influences which are so often unpredictable and can upset the most carefully laid plans for investment.

If the City of London is sometimes thought to be too cautious in looking to the future, I believe that this attitude helps to create and to account for the great financial strength which enables us to meet our commitments, large and small and whenever they fall due, over long periods.

7

Behind the Figures

You could have knocked me down with the proverbial feather when an elderly American widow suddenly asked, 'Do you hold any I.B.M.s and are they going to split?' I had been introduced to the lady on the deck of the *Queen Mary*, we had been talking about French architecture, but I found that she read the *Wall Street Journal* and was nearly as well informed on the prospects for the shares of International Business Machines Inc. as were many brokers I had seen in Wall Street. 'Splitting', by the way, is American for issuing free bonus shares to a stockholder in proportion to the number of shares he already holds. A vast amount of capital is owned by American widows (who are apt to be a menace to their bank managers), but I relate this incident to illustrate the widespread knowledge of finance which prevails across the Atlantic. Perhaps they go to one extreme. We certainly go to the other, and those of us who hold investments are inclined to throw the reports which announce our dividends into the wastepaper basket, unless it is to criticize them as 'too dull for words' or as 'extravagantly printed'—a comment I have heard several times when coloured photographs have appeared to liven up the figures. There is, however, a happy mean, and in recent years I have issued supplements to our Institution's accounts to explain what is behind the annual figures of a life assurance company.

Everyone likes to have some 'savings', but it has been aptly said that when they belong to someone else—and especially if they are large in amount—they at once become 'capital', with all the opprobrium attaching to the term. Saving conjures up a host of virtues; capital is liable to various forms of political attention during the lifetime of its owner, and may eventually disappear in death duties. Perhaps the term first became odious in the context of the Industrial Revolution, and the same feeling was encouraged during the depression in the nineteen-thirties when men appeared to matter less than money. But all that is now past history: in looking back I believe we should always take account of the mental climate of the time, and a generation which sent its children to bed on the slightest pretext without any supper did not at first see that it was cruel to send boys up chimneys or women down the mines. Perhaps later generations will condemn us for requiring children of five to attend school all day and for filling their minds out of school with theft and murder on television. However that may be, capital is more than ever needed to finance the projects of a new scientific age, and it is important to understand how the money we are saving in one way or another is being put to work and what lies behind the figures by which commerce of all kinds is measured.

My father remarked in *The Confessions of a Capitalist* that if we eat the whole crop of potatoes there will be none left for seed to provide next year's supply and that in essence the role of capital is as simple as that—it represents resources withheld from current consumption in order to provide for the needs of tomorrow. While this kind of point is taken for granted by economists, it is seldom expressed in simple terms for the benefit of the man in the street; in the same way there is a need to break down the big figures relating to the national economy into units which the ordinary citizen can understand.

An excellent example of what I may term popular economics was provided by the chairman of the Westminster Bank at its annual meeting a few years ago. Discussing the balance of payments problem and the loss of gold reserves, Lord Aldenham said that if during 1955 the 50 million people in these islands had each spent £5 less on themselves, loss of gold reserves could on certain conditions have been avoided. I am not competent to discuss the technical basis of this calculation, but it shows clearly how comparatively small savings make a vital contribution to the national balance sheet. And since life assurance is now the largest channel for personal savings, I may add that, as against the hypothetical figure of £5 per head, actual savings entrusted to the United Kingdom Provident Institution in the same year in the form of premiums on new assurances averaged £45 per policyholder. And the policyholder is a man or woman who has undertaken to go on saving in the future.

* * * * *

These figures bring out in a striking way how much the economy depends on small savings, and this brings me to the part played by the industrial assurance companies who collect and invest such vast sums today. Their policyholders are, of course, all capitalists, so are the contributors to trade unions' funds, pensions schemes and so on, who have a stake in the country provided by the shillings and pence which they regularly pay in dues and premiums. The industrial assurance companies collect the premiums at the door, usually once a week, a method which distinguishes this type of insurance from the kind conducted by what are termed 'ordinary' offices. In the latter type of business the onus is on the policy-holder to pay the premium, which is done through the post usually on an annual basis.

When insurance was first featured in the plans of the Labour Party, it was proposed to nationalize those companies which did any industrial business—it was suggested that the small weekly sums involved should be paid instead to the State to become part of the National Insurance system. Soon after the Labour intentions were announced, the chairman of one of the leading industrial companies said that it would be an 'illuminating experience' if members of his audience could spend a day with one of the company's collectors. I therefore wrote to ask if I might take advantage, incognito, of his suggestion, and one morning in September, 1949, I reported at a suburban office as a 'friend of the General Manager' interested in the nationalization issue and the public reaction to it. The manager predicted that the subject was most unlikely to come up in the course of the morning's round, and he proved to be right. But from some thirty calls at addresses ranging from council flats and prefabs to shops, public houses and an expensive private nursing-home, I gained an insight into industrial assurance that was of intense interest. No doubt larger policies are now being taken out than in 1949 and the payments and sums assured would be larger than those I shall now describe.

The collector I accompanied had on his book 600 clients, whose average payment was 1s 4d weekly on a £50 policy, and whose average income, so far as it is possible to generalize, was at that time about £6 a week. Payments are made weekly, fortnightly or monthly, and I was struck by the high percentage of individuals who are paying on two, three or four policies, usually for relatives (in some cases abroad) or for lodgers. Several of the poorest in appearance produced a pound note to pay premiums of two or three shillings. As mentioned earlier, industrial is distinguished from general insurance by the collection of premiums at the door, in contrast with their transmission by the insured through the post or a bank. There are limits and conditions prescribed by law as to the amounts which may be handled, but anyone who imagines that collectors have to extract payments from an unwilling public should watch a collector at work.

I was frankly surprised by the welcome which Mr Smith, as I shall name him, everywhere received. Some of his clients were waiting on the doorstep with the money, others chaffed him for being a little ahead of his usual time, or a little late. At some houses he looked under the mat, or perhaps in a tin, where the receipt book and the money had been left ready for him. In one case it was put at the bottom of the stairs, and in taking the change upstairs to the householder the collector also carried up the milk! The friendly greeting was the same, even when the householder 'could not afford to pay this week', as happened where a family had just returned from holiday and, as one working woman put it, 'had not had time to turn round'. Mr Smith told me as we walked away that he could trust that particular client for six months and feel sure of payment. In another case where a £500 policy of a City clerk was in arrear, the collector was invited by the wife to come in tomorrow evening when her husband would be at home to discuss how best they could 'straighten things out'. I learned that an illness had upset the family budget, but the collector felt sure they would make good, so keen was this particular couple to maintain their insurance.

What, I asked, was the aim of the average insured person in this locality? What was the proportion of whole life and endowment policies? Among the elderly, chiefly widows living on pensions or with help from a son or daughter, a 'decent funeral' was frankly the main concern. I was told that many of these old people were extremely interested in what would happen on their death, and that the £20 provided under National Insurance had made little difference, since it was considered quite inadequate. In the early days of the State scheme many old people were not eligible for the funeral grant, and their weekly payments to the industrial insurance offices had been put by year by year to provide for this inevitable contingency. A claim is normally settled within forty-eight hours of death, payment being made by the collector who knows the personal circumstances and can advise the relatives on the funeral and other formalities. The legal delays involved in the case of larger estates seldom arise among industrial insurers. Most younger folk now divide their payments between endowment and death benefits, taking advantage of both types of policy. Much of the business is with married couples, but many young women are taking out policies, and since they earn more as typists or shop assistants than the black-coated male worker of the same age, they are among Mr Smith's best 'prospects'.

On entering one top-floor flat I found that the seventy-year-old occupant was a reader both of *Punch* and the *Journal of the Royal Horticultural Society*! She explained that Mr Smith was lucky to have caught her in. Since his last visit a month ago she had been to France and to Salisbury, and was shortly going to see her brother in Wales. I asked the collector why this woman did not take out an ordinary policy instead of paying out small sums. It seemed that she had had a legacy, but from force of careful habit preferred to continue the instalments.

A publican handed out more than a pound on his books, which proved to be for industrial policies on the lives of his brother and sister. He himself was insured for £1,000 under an ordinary policy. The tenant of a prefab asked for advice on the purchase of a house—what would the deposit and instalments amount to? Knowing the husband's age already, Mr Smith was able to quote immediate terms. In another case a shop proprietor had just acquired a motor cycle, and Mr Smith asked to have the insurance but proved to be too late. His biggest 'prospect' was the secretary of a nursing-home who had just bought a television set and a piano, and wanted them insured before she went on holiday. Other cases which stand out from the many I saw included that of a young widow with four children. Her late husband, many years older, had always declined insurance proposals, but she had made a start in his lifetime and was now paying premiums for the whole family.

The day was fine and sunny, and from my own experience of 'the road' when I worked in Fleet Street I know what a difference good weather makes both to collector and client. The sunshine served to diminish the aches and pains of some of the elderly folk on whom we called, but Mr Smith clearly brought cheer and encouragement to many who looked forward to his regular visit. I must confess I was depressed, not by evidences of poverty, which were few, but by the prevalence of ailments and the large part they occupy in the thoughts of the elderly poor.

Long before my tour ended it was obvious to me that the collector was 'guide, philosopher and friend' to his clients, and that the community would be the loser if he were replaced by a Government official, however kindly he might be, since no State monopoly would be likely to allow the discretion and latitude which are at present such marked features of this widespread method of saving.

* * * * *

Although the sums collected in the way I have just described are for the most part small, they add up to very big figures as so many people all over the country are saving week by week through industrial assurance. Taking the business of all the life companies into account, millions of pounds are collected every year, and as mentioned on earlier pages, their investment makes a very important contribution to the capital requirements of British industry. In 1958 all forms of saving are much greater than a few years ago, and issues of new capital are meeting with a ready and adequate response. But as recently as 1951-52 the position was very different, and insurance money was then the major—perhaps the only—source of new money for industry. An authority outside the insurance world, Lord Sinclair, stated that by 1951 industry from its own profits was 'not strengthening its resources in any way commensurate with its task in expanding production', and he added: 'It is clear that in 1951 insurance and pension funds were the main outside source of such net capital formation as there was.' As the United Kingdom Provident Institution had been a pioneer in investing in ordinary shares, I urged that the life offices generally should provide more risk capital when this step was looked upon with extreme caution, and it is satisfactory to note that in the last few years even larger amounts have been made available to industry in this way.

The days of the large private investor may be over, but

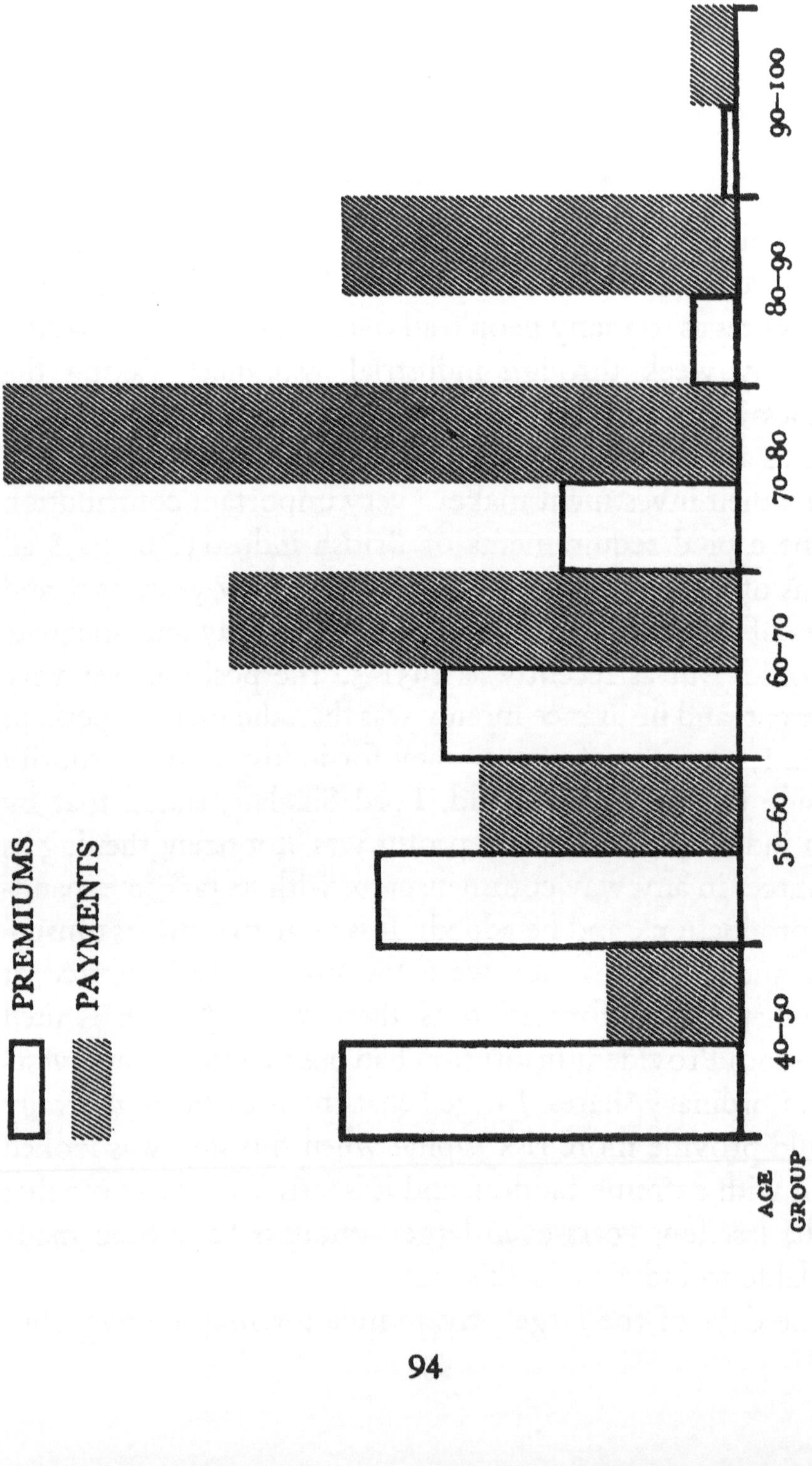

WHY LARGE FUNDS ARE HELD BY A LIFE ASSURANCE COMPANY

more and more people are now acquiring a financial stake in the country by means of life assurance funds. Not long ago the assets of 44 leading offices were valued at over £4,400 millions and there is a great variety in the disposal of their investments. For instance, one office has 41 per cent of its assets in Government stocks, another as little as 9 per cent. The proportions in ordinary shares range from 38 per cent to 4 per cent, while one office has no less than 26 per cent of its investments in property against an average of 8·7.

As these funds are growing at the rate of about 8 per cent a year, it is important that the public should understand the indispensable part which they play in the life assurance business. At present we are often criticized for holding them, and even some of those who are well disposed towards us are inclined to think that our resources are far larger than they need be. My own office therefore issued a publication a few years ago entitled *Our Policy—And Yours* to give the policyholder an explanation of this subject. Large funds are held by a life office, we explained, to meet commitments to policyholders, but these funds are different from the reserves of an ordinary business undertaking which are put aside to meet essential requirements, such as maintenance of machinery and stocks, and as a protection against bad times. The life office funds are the amount of money estimated to be necessary and actually held to pay the full sums assured as and when they become due, provided that this money is kept invested at a satisfactory rate of interest. Their essential role can be illustrated by relating the premiums received and the payments to members in successive periods. For example, if a number of whole-life assurances are taken out at age 40, payments made by the life office as deaths occur during successive periods of ten years will normally follow the pattern of the diagram on page 94, in which the premiums received and the payments made during each period are shown in white and shaded rectangles.

It will be seen that there is a surplus of premiums over payments during the first twenty years but thereafter the outgo exceeds the income to an increasing extent. This difference can only be met if the excess premiums received in the early years are invested and accumulated with interest, and over 40 per cent of our gross income is now derived from interest. The total accumulations held for these and other types of policies make up the funds shown in the accounts, and the size of these funds is a measure of the commitments which we shall be called upon to meet in the future. In the case of our particular institution whose funds now exceed £50 million, the average stake of our policyholders at the present time is about £600.

8

Measuring Success

Every schoolboy associates the City of London with Tower Bridge, the Lord Mayor's Show—and Dick Whittington! We all hope to see the bridge open, but as this happens on an average only once in three hours, few of us realize our ambition. Adult feelings about the Lord Mayor's Show depend on whether we work in the City or not. At some time or another every family within striking distance goes to see this historic spectacle which dates from mediaeval times, and as we get older we think it is not as good as it used to be. If our office is on the route, it provides a good excuse for a party; if not, we curse the traffic jams and agree with the periodic suggestion that the Show should take place on a Saturday. Yet there would doubtless be an uproar if a serious attempt was made to abolish it. The City has witnessed all kinds of processions through many centuries, and its special status is recognized whenever the King or Queen enters its boundaries and is met by the Lord Mayor at Temple Bar, in Fleet Street. There, the Lord Mayor hands a jewelled sword to the Monarch, who at once hands it back and thereby attests to the City's ancient rights and independence.

Popular feelings about Dick Whittington are of another kind. Everyone loves a success story, and of course his cat is a favourite in the pantomime season. As Whittington was the son of a wealthy citizen, he was not the poor boy of popular romance, but it seems quite likely that he was treated badly by the cook and ran away from home, after giving his cat to a ship's captain bound for Barbary. Legend has it that when he got to Bunhill Fields the bells of Bow Church seemed to say,

'Turn again, Whittington
Thrice Mayor of London',

and that treasures worth £100,000 were sent by the King of Barbary in exchange for the cat, so making Dick the richest commoner in the land. But as a matter of history, Sir Richard Whittington did become Lord Mayor three times and a great benefactor of the City. In 1400 he rebuilt the Church of St Michael Paternoster, he began to rebuild Newgate Prison, and left money in his Will to repair St Bartholomew's Hospital.

The wealth of the City has long been proverbial, and fortunes have been made there all through the centuries. Side by side with many worthy merchants, some others have shown what a writer in 1866 called 'very selfish energy and very wordly wisdom'[1]; and since both religion and philosophy have harsh things to say about money, it is hardly surprising that many people are confused about this whole subject.

* * * * *

When I went to Harrow forty years ago, a parent who happened to be in business would often describe himself on his son's entry form as a director of companies. During my

[1] *English Merchants* by H. R. Fox Bourne (Chatto & Windus, 1866).

first term I shared a room with an Anglo-South African whose father had made a fortune with Cecil Rhodes. There was a suggestion of Empire-building about diamonds, but towards business in general a conspiracy of silence prevailed. Snobbery contributed to this attitude, but it also reflected certain other considerations, for, after all, Plato had said that the influence of trading was morally corrupting; Xenophon deplored the 'vulgar crafts'. Every history lesson pointed to a career in the Services or professions and with the exception of *Jerry*, who on leaving Harrow

> 'Tramps to his desk with a swing
> Bearing the orthodox bag . . .'

all our school songs were in praise of the public life.

At a time when education and wealth often went together it was natural that money was not a subject of conversation; like one's underclothes, it was assumed to be there. Many public school boys then came of wealthy families, while those who did not were assured of an income in the professions which were only open to educated men. There was therefore nothing particularly high-minded in the attitude to money, but in the circumstances the emphasis was on the job rather than the remuneration. Today, the whole scene has of course changed. Public schools have careers masters, and many firms send representatives to recruit senior boys for business and industry. Yet while pay and prospects are obviously important I believe that the traditional sense of values still has a salutary influence, and this is certainly true of the City.

Englishmen are reluctant to discuss motives and I rather liked the comment of a sturdy banker friend of mine who, when listening to a speaker talking on these lines, said,

'Nonsense! We are simply making a living like everyone else'. Yet I have risked a lapse from the accepted code and am quite ready to be charged with moralizing, because it needs to be emphasized that dealing in money involves an intensely professional sense which is jealously guarded by those who work in the City of London.

The plain fact is that very few people understand the function of money-making in trade and business, which are at the mercy of supply and demand, competition, new materials, inventions, fashion, climate, and of course, Parliament. So, unlike the pay of the soldier, the earnings of business can seldom be taken for granted.

For those who do not work in the City, nothing is harder to understand than that the City man deals with money in just the same way that a grocer handles sugar or a builder lays bricks. In its various forms, money has characteristics which can be assessed like those of any other material, and as already mentioned is subject to the various factors which govern business of other kinds. After spending twenty years in publishing, and being occupied every day with paper and print, I still find it hard to realize that the bankers and brokers and financiers with whom I now associate in the City have the same objective approach to their raw material as I had to the various products which go into the making of a book.

A business man in deciding whether to embark on a new line has to find out what other similar articles are available, he must gauge the likely demand, and decide whether it can be produced at a price which the public will pay. Suppose an article is under consideration of which it will cost £100 to manufacture 1,000. Ignoring for the sake of simplicity overheads, retailers' discounts, etc., the actual cost will then be 2s od per article. If the whole quantity is sold, the manufacturer will get his money back, but as the exact demand can seldom be forecast he will probably base his calculations on a quantity of 800 and price them at 2s 6d. If less than 800 are sold there will be a loss, if more a profit, and so the money made is a measure of the success or failure of this particular venture.

Similar considerations apply to a City transaction. An issuing house which has been asked to raise new capital for an industrial firm, for example, must go into its record and prospects in great detail. Manufacturing and marketing factors must be investigated; the right terms to attract the investor at the moment of the issue must be gauged; this in turn involves the money market and other wider considerations. Altogether the whole process is highly technical. The terms are made as attractive as possible to the investor, as there is always the risk that the price of the shares may prove too dear on the day the issue is advertised in the newspapers, because of some change in the overall financial or economic conditions, which govern the price factor in the City as sensitively as the weather governs the mercury in a barometer. Even such a 'safe' and staid affair as a corporation stock can fail, as has happened in the case of several recent issues. The terms are normally submitted in advance to underwriters, whose function I described in an earlier chapter, and sometimes the terms may then be modified.

Just as an active publisher is constantly looking for new and attractive books, so a financial firm must offer new services if its business is to progress. Every business undertaking must expand or decline—it can seldom mark time for long—and the keen eye for sales which prompts a car maker to offer coachwork in two colours instead of one prompts a banker to launch a Personal Cheque scheme or to sponsor a new Unit Trust. The success of the venture is normally reflected in the profit made, but in the eyes of the promoters the emphasis is on success and this leads them to offer the public the most attractive terms compatible with sound finance. Contrary to a popular misconception, the question is not how much profit can be squeezed out of a particular transaction but on how fine a margin can it be carried through. To say this is not to deny that financiers want to make money; it simply puts the whole process in perspective.

The City is very much aware that in a free society which allows a choice of goods and services, business must pay its way or go under. This applies to a small firm of stockbrokers or a large insurance company, with the difference that any well-established concern with strong reserves can more easily ride a storm or come through a period of depression. A State undertaking can be run at a loss so long as the Government is prepared to subsidize it from the taxes, most of which come from profits made in other sectors of the economy, but in all forms of free-enterprise business, the making or losing of money is the ultimate measure of success or failure. However admirable a commodity or service may be in the eyes of its producer, the commercial test is whether someone else is prepared to pay for it. In common with the grocer, the builder and the publisher, an insurance company must keep its charges or premium rates as low as possible in a competitive market, which means that the costs of selling policies and administering the office must be constantly watched, while at the same time, as has been shown elsewhere in this book, the money entrusted to the company must be invested to the best advantage. If an insurance company were to become careless or extravagant, or failed to pursue an active and skilful investment policy its revenues would suffer and people would soon buy their policies from a rival office. All of which is obvious when stated in this simple way but is apt to be overlooked when a critic starts to talk about the wealth of the City, as if this either does not have to be earned, or is in some way made at the expense of the public.

* * * * *

To turn from the general to the particular, in British life-assurance practice the profits distributed to holders of with-profit policies are generally in the form of an addition to the original sum assured. This is called a bonus (meaning *good* in Latin), and can take one of several forms. The bonus is normally retained by the company until the policy matures, when it reverts to the policyholder along with the original sum assured, and is therefore referred to as reversionary. Some bonuses are also called compound, because they are calculated on the sum assured as increased by previous bonuses as distinct from a simple bonus calculated on the original sum assured only. Many kinds of assurance are available either as a policy sharing in profits or without profits. Under both types the sum assured is guaranteed but the policy with profits naturally costs rather more in premiums to secure this added benefit.

As the bonus represents profits, one might expect that it would be paid at once in cash. In the United States it usually is, and so is referred to over there as a dividend. But under British practice, since the object of a with-profit policy is to provide an increasing amount of life cover, profits are normally distributed in the form of additional assurance. Bonuses are usually declared at the end of every three or five years, so that the value of the policy increases at these intervals.

Where does the profit come from? Premium rates, as already mentioned, have to be fixed at the outset for policies which will run for a long time ahead and must take account of the claims expected to arise, the expenses of running the business, and the interest likely to be earned on the invested premiums. When the net results under these heads are better than the estimates, there is a balance or profit which helps to provide the bonus. In practice the most potent factor is the interest rate, which, despite rising costs since the war, has been reflected in the steadily increasing bonus paid by many offices.

How is the amount determined? Parliament has laid down that an actuarial investigation must be made at least every five years to determine the amount which a life office must have in hand to meet claims as they become due, taking into account the premiums still to come and the interest to be obtained by the investment of the funds in future years. Many offices have found it advantageous to make the investigation every third year, when the valuation results are notified to members with the usual annual report. The amount by which the actual funds exceed the sums shown to be necessary by the valuation is referred to as the 'surplus'. The directors may consider it prudent to retain part of this to meet future contingencies not otherwise provided for; the rest is used to provide the bonus. By increasing the original sum assured the bonus helps to counter any fall in the value of money during the lifetime of the policy, while the income tax relief allowed on premiums is a further attraction. Clearly, the bonus offers a strong incentive to save, for unlike a dividend from an ordinary investment which is at once distributed and often spent, the bonus is reinvested for the future benefit of the policyholder and goes on producing further income.

Since stability and continuity are such important factors in this business, the law does not require life offices to publish the market value of their assets, but, like the banks, they are allowed to hold inner reserves, sometimes called 'hidden' reserves. This suggests an air of mystery, but they are simply the difference between the price at which investments and other assets stand in the books and their market value at the time the accounts are made up and published. We make profits and sometimes losses from buying and selling investments, but these transactions are purely incidental. In the long run it is mainly to income that we must look to carry on our business profitably, and so ensure having a surplus from which to pay the bonus. The appreciation that may occur in the value of our assets does not of itself increase income and it is liable to melt away, as the ups and downs on the Stock Exchange often show in a spectacular way. Its chief and most valuable function is to protect income—and surplus—by providing capital reserves from which capital losses, which would otherwise fall on income, can be met. Looking back on the experience of my own Institution, the balance sheets show that for many years we were faced with depreciation, and from 1895 to 1920 it was necessary to provide out of revenue for a fall in the value of our assets on no fewer than thirteen occasions. Even as late as 1938 there was very little appreciation to show, but since the war the position has steadily improved. It will be seen that over long periods the 'hidden' reserves enable a life office to pursue a steady course. The funds respond to fluctuations in the market, but these reserves help us to meet the claims of policyholders and to add the good measure of profit by which the success of our particular form of business has been judged for well over a century.

* * * * *

Talking with friends outside the City, I find that the whole subject of reserves—and not only so-called hidden reserves—is apt to be puzzling, and not long ago a friend of mine who is an architect said he was left completely baffled by the accounts of a housing company of which we are fellow-directors. A day or two later I wrote to him as follows:

Your very proper question about the accounts at the Cottage Company meeting caught me unawares; and as much for my own edification as (I hope) for yours, I shall now try to put a clear answer on paper.

There are, of course, two statements which a company presents annually to its shareholders: (1) the Profit and Loss Account, showing the income and expenditure during the year under review; and (2) the Balance Sheet, giving an overall picture of the company's position at the close of the year.

In the case of the Cottage Company, the revenue comes from rents and from any profits made on the sale of houses, while on the expenditure side the heaviest items are repairs and maintenance. The draft Profit and Loss Account for the year circulated by the auditor showed that expenses exceeded revenue by £100. At the close of the previous year, however, there was a 'carry forward' of £113. You will find this figure at the foot of the account on the revenue side, and after setting against this the present year's loss, we were left with a carry forward of £13.

You therefore asked: 'Well, how can a dividend of nearly

£300 be paid if we have lost money and only have £13 to carry forward? Can you change the position merely by bookkeeping?'

These questions bring us to (2), the Balance Sheet.

When the Company was first launched a number of people put up money in varying amounts to buy land and build houses. They received in return share certificates, which put on record that Mr A (Mrs B, etc.) owns a share of the property proportionate to the money he (or she) has invested. The Company then owes these shareholders the amount of its capital—hence Share Capital appears as the first item on the 'liability' side of the Balance Sheet. On the 'asset' side—to balance this—the first item is land and buildings.

For simplicity, let us assume the capital is £10,000 and is all spent on ten houses which cost exactly £10,000. The Balance Sheet would then show:

Share Capital	£10,000	Land & Buildings	£10,000

Let us also assume that very soon one of these houses is sold for £1,200 at a profit of £200 which finds its way into the Profit and Loss Account. This profit belongs to the shareholders, so the Company's liability is increased by £200 and this item is therefore shown next on the liability side of the Balance Sheet.

The picture will then be as follows:

Share Capital	£10,000	Land & Buildings	£9,000
Profit & Loss A/c	200	Cash	1,200
	£10,200		£10,200

In course of time further profits are earned and instead of being retained in cash are spent on more land and houses.

The profit is still there, although now it is chiefly represented by bricks and mortar. At this point, the directors will probably decide to create a Reserve Account—to withdraw some of the profits from the Profit and Loss Account (i.e. from current use) and put them by for a rainy day or some special purpose. This Reserve Account then appears as the next item on the liability side of the Balance Sheet, the Company being liable to the shareholders for the extra asset so represented. The Balance Sheet will then look like this:

Share Capital	£10,000	Land & Building	£11,500
Profit & Loss A/c	200		
Reserve Account	2,000	Cash (say)	700
	£12,200		£12,200

You will see clearly that the reserves are not necessarily in cash or liquid assets, but they are a measure of successful trading in previous years and represent value (ultimately realizable) just the same.

Applying all this to the Cottage Company's latest annual account, the directors agreed to transfer £1,000 from reserves to Profit and Loss Account, and to pay the dividend out of reserves, which is permitted provided that this fact is fully disclosed to the shareholders. As the company holds more than £600 in cash, and the dividend will require less than £300, the cash position presents no problem. You will now understand that there is no 'wangle', we are simply taking something from the larder to help to keep the finances of the company on an even keel after what has proved to be a difficult year.

III

A WIDER VIEW

9

Theory and Practice

Having shown the reader something of the business of a City institution and how we put money to work, it is time to take a wider view. Hardly a day passes without some new proposal affecting business coming from one or other of the political parties, and Conservative as well as Labour Governments are giving the City their active attention. During the 1951 election when the Labour Party returned to the subject of dividend limitation, the Conservatives took up the idea, and *The Times* said there was 'no escaping the fact that both parties are after the investor of risk capital with a carving knife'.

'The bitter pill that the investor has to swallow', this newspaper added, 'is that evidently both the big parties believe that an actual majority of the electors favour acts of hostility towards risk-capital. Moreover, since neither party can conceivably believe that the minute redistribution of incomes or taxes resulting from their proposals would directly add anything noticeable to the poorer wage-earner's material welfare, quite apart from the indirect dangers it involves, they must believe that a majority either are under the illusion that there is a large and luscious cake to be carved up or are in favour of mere negative spite. This interpretation of the popular attitude does not accord with everybody's ordinary experience of his fellow-men. But the parties are expert in their field of study; and that is what they think. If they are right, there is room for an effort to educate a wider public on the issues at stake. The parties themselves might try to elaborate their arguments and to find the real principles at issue, as they do with great care and in great detail on many subjects less fundamentally important.'

The Labour Party is apt to attack the City because it is associated with capitalism, and of course by the same token many Conservatives regard socialism as the arch enemy. Two of my City friends were recently discussing this important topic. One said that another Labour administration would be the 'final blow' to the capitalist system, the other thought it would not make much difference since, in the well-known phrase, 'we are all socialists now'. But what I have seen myself during thirty years of great change suggests that theory and practice are seldom the same thing, and that the City and the business community as a whole will have to look well beyond the orthodox party struggle if an effective 'public relations' policy is to be framed for the years ahead.

With these thoughts in mind, I propose in the present chapter to leave the City for a while and to devote a few pages to a mining village in South-West Durham twenty years ago. Our personal politics are influenced by upbringing to a greater extent than most of us realize, and like many privileged persons, until I saw heavy unemployment at first hand I held 'right wing' views. But experience in the distressed areas forced me to do some hard thinking on political issues, which is relevant to the situation facing the City of London today.

* * * * *

'If the eagerness of the men for work and the commercial possibilities were really appreciated in the prosperous South,' I wrote in the *Daily Telegraph* in November, 1937, 'the express trains to Wales and Durham would be packed with business visitors, anxious to do their bit in solving one of the most baffling problems of the present time.' A few months previously Parliament had provided financial inducements to industry to establish new factories in districts where unemployment was as high as 30 per cent. Until then the powers of the Commissioner for the Special Areas, Sir Malcolm Stewart, had been limited to public works and charity and he concluded that persuasion alone had proved 'futile' in getting manufacturers to go to the distressed areas.

My optimism was sustained by what I had seen at a mining village in South-West Durham, where excellent factory sites were available, morale was still high, and a local committee representing all sections of the community was making strenuous efforts to solve a tragic problem. A letter had reached me from South-West Durham which read: 'As a doctor I come into contact with unemployed men every day, and I know how great is the desire for work. Many of the younger men suffer from neurasthenia, due to prolonged idleness and worry. If you are likely to be in the North, why not come and visit this area?' I met the doctor some days later in Newcastle, and found him to be a man of vision and energy, with a big practice in a mining town of 30,000 people. About a third were out of work, but many new houses had been built before the depression and the town had good amenities to offer. The next step was a meeting in the town hall, at which a committee was formed representing all sections of opinion and including a surveyor, accountant and bank manager who would be in a position to advise on local business prospects. Having secured particulars of the available buildings, we sent an attractive circular headed 'Wanted Six New Industries' to selected firms in several trades and also to the newspapers.

As a result of this propaganda several business men visited Durham. There was a young importer of Swedish furniture, who was considering manufacturing in England; but eventually he decided to go back into a different line of business in which he had been trained. Another manufacturer of furniture arranged a visit, but unfortunately his fellow-directors would not sanction a new factory. A brick and tile manufacturer with a chain of brickworks would undoubtedly have started a branch if the local sand had proved suitable. Enquiries were usually followed up by a personal interview. One London manufacturer told me that it was an insult to ask him to go to a Special Area unless the Government would train the men, and he would not listen to the argument that he might train them himself by sending down a few selected men from London, as was being done by some other new firms on Tyneside. A promising enquiry came from a foreign firm, and three engineers spent a week-end in the snow with the doctor examining a likely site, but firms in the City were not prepared to finance the project.

Success eventually came through the enterprise of a joinery manufacturer, who besides being a keen business man was evidently a philanthropist, for he had built houses for his workmen in the Home Counties. He wanted another factory in the North and during his first visit to Durham paid the deposit on a site of ten acres. The factory was built in record time with the aid of a large loan from the Nuffield Trust, and very soon fifty men were employed. On the principle that every little helped, this was very satisfactory, but while several hundred factories were built with Government aid in the Special Areas as a whole, and many small firms showed great enthusiasm, the numbers employed were very modest in relation to the immense unemployment problem of the period.

The whole episode convinced me that more vigorous measures were needed and that the Government should step in in a really big way. An embargo on further factories in the London area was an obvious step that should have been taken.[1] 'Older men might well be employed on digging underground garages for use in air raid emergencies on a big scale' was another measure I suggested in the *Daily Telegraph*. By then, of course, the war clouds were beginning to gather, in September, 1939, and the whole problem was resolved by the urgent need for men and guns.

* * * * *

If free enterprise did not prove able to solve the mass unemployment of the 'thirties, the red tape involved in official measures was another retarding factor. Although now commonplace, it was then an entirely new experience, and all that I learnt in dealing with official agencies showed the need for a drastic speeding up and a very different attitude. This led me to suggest that future Government grants for the areas should be put into the hands of public spirited business men, such as the Nuffield Trustees for the Special Areas. As a rule the Trustees lent money in the form of 4 per cent debentures, making a condition that the promoter should himself put up about 30 per cent of the

[1] Measures of this kind were announced by the Government in July, 1958, to encourage industry to go into coastal and other areas where local unemployment is beginning to be a problem again.

capital to be repaid in five years, and in the short space of eighteen months they disposed of £2,000,000.

By contrast the Special Areas Reconstruction Association, from which I tried to get a loan of only £1,000 for a coal-briquetting scheme, was very slow to deal with, and the same impression was formed from my contacts with the South-West Durham Development Board, another Government agency. In one case a tailor at Bishop Auckland who had qualified for Army clothing contracts, but had not sufficient capital to buy more machinery, was refused a loan of £5,000 after his application had been in hand for six months. At the trading estates established under Government auspices near Cardiff, Newcastle and Glasgow, the help given by local business men to the officials concerned had been immensely valuable, and I therefore strongly opposed a suggestion that the Special Commissoner's powers should be taken over by the Board of Trade.

All these views were formed when nationalization was still a theory. A further passage from my diary now seems to explain why this theory would nevertheless be put into practice directly the war was over, with memories of the heavy unemployment of the 'thirties still so vivid in the minds of the electorate:

'As hundreds of good men remain idle, through the lack of opportunity which business men are best qualified to give, it is not surprising that opponents of private enterprise say that the State must take industry over, lock, stock and barrel. . . . Unless, however, private enterprise will rise to the occasion without further delay the Commissioner may be forced to seek powers to conduct (and not merely to construct) factories in particular trades suited to each locality. This would be a radical step, but the problem is too serious for any method which will help its solution to be ruled out. As a business man I dislike the principle of Government trading, but unless we do our job we cannot complain if the State fills in the gaps.'

* * * * *

When, in due course, the time came for the State to step into the affairs of business and industry in a big way after the General Election of 1945, the City entered a period of constant strain and uncertainty, and we never quite knew what Parliament was going to do next. With good humour and patience the City adapted itself to new ideas and regulations, while at the same time having grave misgivings about some of the changes involved such as bulk buying by Government departments and the arbitrary technique of the Capital Issues Committee. Once again the difficulties confronting us in attempting to satisfy political theory were shown during the General Election of 1951, when, as already mentioned, both the political parties put forward proposals affecting risk capital. Since the return to Conservative rule, the skill and experience of the City have had increasing freedom to prove their value to the country, but nevertheless it is clear that much Government activity in the economic sphere is here to stay, whatever the complexion of future Parliaments may be.

As I am trying, in this chapter, to show that extreme views of any kind do not appeal to Englishmen for very long, I shall mention one other personal experience which is relevant to the argument. My address as a National Conservative candidate to the electors of North Bradford, issued before polling day on July 5, 1945, deplored a narrow party approach to current problems as both 'harmful and misleading' and added: 'I do not believe that the future will see 100 per cent individualism or 100 per cent socialism in England, where the sturdy independence and sense of neighbourliness combined in our national character enable us to avoid the extremes of violent disunity found in some other countries'.

After the result of the poll had been announced,[1] I suggested as the defeated candidate that the Conservatives in Parliament, without wavering in their belief in free enterprise, 'should bring constructive criticism to bear on the proposals for nationalization and not merely obstruct them. . . . Liberty and nationalization will be very difficult to reconcile and if the people find themselves subjected to excessive control and regimentation they will vote to restore their freedom at the first opportunity.'

Events since 1945 afford no reason for altering these views; and if I find myself less than ever inclined to be dogmatic I notice that the second report of the Cohen Committee, published in August, 1958, underlines the need for an open-minded approach to the problems ahead. Since the 'Three Wise Men' comprising this committee are popularly regarded as orthodox and right wing—they were boycotted by the T.U.C.—the following passage is all the more significant. The Committee declares that 'To maintain high and stable employment while avoiding inflation, if it is possible at all, will certainly call for a rather delicate regulation of the general level of activity. It is far from certain that our present understanding of the working of economic forces is sufficient for such a purpose. Research could no doubt gradually enlarge that understanding, though it is not to be

[1] *Bradford North,* Nichol, Mrs W. M. (Lab) 20,268; Benn, J. (C) 16,824; Town, R. W. (L) 9,337.

supposed that there is any quick way to answer the hardest and most important questions.'

This statement is reminiscent of the views of the Londoners of 1619 quoted in an earlier chapter, and seems to suggest that, three centuries later, we are still feeling our way.

Naturally, most business men are anti-socialist. No enterprising firm wants to see its operations taken over by the State, and a self-respecting industry can hardly keep silent if it is directly challenged from any political quarter, but our first task is to be sure that our own house is in order. We should be asking ourselves whether we have an effective answer in terms of free enterprise in 1958 to the problems which led so many, in 1938, to believe that the State should step in. Would free enterprise really rise to the occasion if the same situation arose again and take the lead in providing fresh employment instead of putting the onus on the Government? And have we really thought out a constructive answer to the problems of redundancy, whether due to slackening of trade or to new processes? Some big industrial firms are dealing with changing conditions in a planned and orderly way, but redundancy still needs a lot of thought before industry as a whole can feel satisfied about the future. By the same token, of course, the opponents of capitalism should ask themselves how they propose to run State industries at a loss without the support which at present comes from taxing the profits of successful free enterprise? After ten years of nationalization this is becoming a very urgent question.

Clearly, the growing concern of the electors with all these problems calls for the fullest information about the activities of business and the City if sound judgment is to be formed and reflected at Westminster. Ignorance is the danger, not change. Events since the war have made it abundantly plain that the City's record in adapting itself to new demands and conditions is second to none. The City of London is still faced with new problems which in some respects are aggravated by the fact that the border line between private and public enterprise is constantly changing. Yet whatever rival theories may suggest, in practice, as an island people dependent on world trade, we are all in the same boat.

10

Paying our Way

The extent to which the private and public sectors of the British economy now intermingle, and the consequences for the City of London, are particularly well illustrated in the experience of the insurance companies. For nearly fifty years, private and State schemes have been running side by side, and steps are now afoot to extend the National Insurance system. The life assurance business is always sensitive to the overall policy of the Government, but since the war we have also been confronted with specific proposals affecting our future. At one stage, part of the insurance industry was marked out for nationalization, and both the main parties in Parliament have now issued plans for State pensions on a wider scale. Ever since 1840 my own life office has faced and met successfully many great changes, but as all parties are now devoting attention to our business I find myself asking just where we stand. How will these developments affect us? Is the Welfare State to become a competitor or a partner? What policy can a life office best adopt in this new situation?

The Welfare Society is not, of course, a new concept. It had a counterpart in Tudor England when the guilds looked after the souls as well as the bodies of their members, and many trades were regulated in great detail. But in our own time the increasing inroads of the Government into business affairs is a new feature, and if we look back to the days when our Institution was getting into its stride the change in the political climate can properly be described as revolutionary. It is difficult to realize today that 'late Victorian politics were for the most part free from material inducements to vote for one party or another. The State was not there to give, but to take and to take as sparingly as possible.' I am quoting Mr R. B. McCallum, the Oxford historian, who describes the position in 1870 in his supplement to Halévy's *Victorian Years*. 'If we ask how an elector could vote to improve himself economically, it is hard to find an answer. There were no tariffs to be put on or removed, no subsidies, no social service benefits. Budgets might vary slightly in the amount of income tax or the price of tea and sugar. . . . Political allegiance was largely a matter of what Bentham would call sympathy and antipathy, of class feeling more than class interest, of religious affinities, of pure political doctrine or simple political sentiment.' Although the vote was still limited, the mass of the people were 'very slow to use their power to seek their own ends'.

As recently as the nineteen-thirties Parliament was still reluctant to intervene in the economic sphere. While several millions remained out of work year after year, even the Opposition in Parliament was timid, by present standards, in calling for drastic remedies. Evidently the hesitation of the Victorian still lingered on in his children, and in support of this view I may perhaps add a postscript to what I have written in the previous chapter. In August, 1936, I suggested that the restriction under which the Special Commissioners could not assist industries 'operating for profit' should be removed, for business must either be run at a profit or loss and in the latter case the area of distress would only be extended. This very moderate proposal was questioned in a leading article in *The Times* on the grounds that a selective subsidy would be hard to justify, while other correspondents expressed concern at the thought of State-aided competition. Eight months later Parliament made history by voting public money for new factories and for loans to private firms. In April, 1937, after more than a month's debate, £2,000,000 were voted for these novel purposes, but continued heavy unemployment encouraged the idea that the nationalization of industry would be a radical change for the better.

Then came the war and its aftermath. For more than ten years the Government took charge of much of the nation's business and we became accustomed to State expenditure running into hundreds of millions. Public money, introduced as a prop to help private business to get on its feet, is now an important factor in several industries, and in those which are nationalized the discipline of profit and loss is not much in evidence. Local authorities are employing direct labour in building houses, schools are being provided with television sets, and we seldom stop to ask whether some new State activity is really necessary, or whether it will damage existing business, or where the money is coming from to pay for it. We put the end first without considering the means, and it is scarcely an exaggeration to say that the State, once looked upon by the mass of the people as the last resort, has now become the first. In retrospect, the £2,000,000 voted to counter unemployment seems a paltry sum, but the pendulum has swung to the other extreme. Government spending is now on a scale which can threaten the stability of the pound, as the various crises since the war, culminating in the crisis of the autumn of 1957, have clearly shown.

* * * * *

Having long urged that the City should influence public opinion on basic issues, I was gratified when, on July 10, 1957, the Chancellor of the Exchequer and the Governor of the Bank of England, Mr Cameron Cobbold, appeared on the same City platform to proclaim the overriding importance of honest money. Some surprise was expressed that the Government's proposals were made known at the opening of my new building in Gracechurch Street instead of first 'in another place'; but, as *The Times* remarked, the fact that people had wished themselves into such a state of expectation before this particular speech was 'a striking measure of the intensity of feeling in the City' on the need to halt inflation. Mr Thorneycroft's speech caught the attention of the whole country, and although his dramatic resignation a few months later embarrassed the Government at what is now seen to have been a critical moment in its fortunes, many of us in the City admired his courage and insistence on the plain fact that we must pay our way or sooner or later the pound will collapse.

'Hardly a day passes', Mr Thorneycroft said, 'without the Government being pressed to spend more money. It is said by high placed military persons that the only form of defence is to have all forms of weapons, ancient and modern. It is said that expenditure on the universities is grotesquely small. It is said that what we spend on roads is quite inadequate. And yet it is said at the same time—incongruously though it may be—that we ought to be dealing more effectively with inflation. You cannot at the same time press on the Government to spend more and ask it to halt inflation. . . . The object must be to secure that these programmes are matched by the savings available or the profits earned, so as to place a less heavy burden on the community. . . . Businesses, local authorities, public boards and private persons, too, must cut their budgets in accordance with the national cloth. Directors and shareholders, bankers and ratepayers will assist the community and themselves if they impress these facts upon one another.'

More than a year later, at the time of writing this chapter, some reduction in industrial activity appears to justify the views of Mr Thorneycroft's critics, who naturally pointed to the danger of reducing capital investment. The Government has once more eased the 'credit squeeze', but only after a solid advance in the gold reserves has been achieved, and unlike the situation in the nineteen-twenties, when a return to the Gold Standard was followed by years of depression, many powerful factors are now pulling in the opposite direction, notably the very high level of Government expenditure. This brings me back to the deeper problems which arise from the generous scale of amenities available under the Welfare State, and to the frame of mind to which they tend to give rise.

In attempting to assess the effects of this new outlook on the future of insurance, I shall deal particularly with pensions, but much of the argument will apply to the future of the business as a whole. Several reports by professional bodies have shown what complex technical issues will face any Government which tackles a new State pensions scheme. Some people argue strongly for such a scheme, others are wholly against it, but as both the main political parties seem bent on something of the kind, the first need is to look for the underlying principles on which the successful practice of insurance must depend, whether undertaken by free enterprise or the State. Much more than the future of a particular business is involved when so much is being done for us by what Herbert Spencer terms 'public instrumentalities'. Over seventy years ago he warned us that the increase in public agencies means that 'each generation is made less familiar with the attainment of desired ends by individual actions'. Clearly we are not just concerned with the result of the next few General Elections—we are dealing with a long-term trend which calls for long-term measures, for as in the past the climate of public opinion will be the deciding influence. I believe that the role of the life offices in encouraging people to stand on their own feet has never been more important than it is today. Every insurance policy is a declaration of independence, a pledge of personal effort, a token of sound finance. Anything approaching a State monopoly of insurance or pensions would be a breach of personal liberty, a basic point that is recognized by all parties in Parliament.

The popular desire for larger and better pensions is, however, a natural outcome of the rising standard of living. The insurance offices are setting the pace and have done much to make the public pension-minded. Far from being enervating, security that is earned can make for peace of mind and better work—very often those who criticize the popular demand for security have never known insecurity themselves. But it needs to be more wisely understood that a pension is a form of deferred pay and that it involves an immediate sacrifice in order that the future may be more secure. The crux of the matter is that pensions, as distinct from State Welfare benefits, must be properly related to the contributions paid. In everyday language, pensions must pay their way.

The first intention of the Government's White Paper on *Provision For Old Age*, to deal with the mounting deficit on National Insurance, is all to the good and, indeed, it is imperative. For while the increase in the weekly contribution introduced early in 1958 covered the extra benefit at the present time, it did not meet the overall cost of these prospective benefits. A married man at the age of 65 would receive benefits of a capital value of £2,650, but if he retired in 1968 he would have paid £550, or in 1978 only £970. In the years ahead, therefore, the gap to be met by the taxpayer would be a steadily growing liability. By drawing public attention to facts like these, the insurance companies can do much to help the cause of sound finance [1] and at the same time to counter the widespread idea that 'someone else will pay'. In the case of the pensions schemes issued by both political parties, the situation illustrates what I believe is the most necessary role of business and the City in face of political developments—to make the facts so clearly known to the people that their intrinsic self-respect and common sense will make itself felt when decisions are recorded at the polls.

The City is, of course, deeply concerned to uphold the principles of sound finance and, whatever form State pensions may eventually assume, it must be obvious to thoughtful people that the first concern of insurance companies is with this underlying factor. Unless we can feel confidence that administrations of all parties will continue to accept this obligation, the new commitments which a life office makes every day to cover long periods ahead would be put in grave jeopardy. When, therefore, a critic of the new scheme alleged in the House of Commons that the Government were proposing to make 'a gift to the

[1] It was satisfactory to note that some announcements on *Politics and Pensions* published in 1958 were short-listed for Mr Punch's Oscar for 'rational and sophisticated advertising'.

insurance companies', he was dealing with what is actually a minor consideration in relation to the great volume of business of all kinds which we conduct. The first requirement in considering proposals to extend State pensions is to look at the picture as a whole.

As about half the employed population in the United Kingdom is now covered by occupational pension schemes, arranged either by the life offices or private pensions funds, I am not alone in questioning the need for any Government to bring in a further State scheme with the subsidies this will inevitably involve. At some future date it is possible that the public will boggle at paying more in State contribution and will vote to reduce such schemes. But at present National Insurance faces a mounting deficit, and since the Government proposes to remedy this by charging people with higher incomes more than would otherwise be necessary to pay for their pensions, I suggest that it would be more honest to describe the new contributions as a Social Security Tax. This is done in America, and avoids confusion with genuine insurance soundly financed on a self-supporting basis. The new British plan has something in common with the Federal Scheme which also includes graded contributions but is operated without subsidies, but even America is already facing problems which seem to be inherent in all Government-sponsored schemes. National Insurance is some twenty-five years older, but the present situation in both countries affords interesting parallels for students of public finance.

★ ★ ★ ★ ★

In capitalist America one might expect an attitude of unqualified opposition to Government schemes of any sort, more especially as Franklin Roosevelt, who launched social security, aroused passions and bitter feelings of the kind once associated in our own country with the name of Lloyd George, and these have not yet faded. Yet with the memories of the great depression of the nineteen-thirties still fresh across the Atlantic, the social security system is undoubtedly there to stay, and the life offices are playing their part in keeping it on sound lines. They are concerned about the future, not for the purpose of opposing the Federal Scheme but on account of the tendency of Governments to go beyond basic needs, to the detriment, as they believe, of the character of the American people and the future of the national economy. To meet the first danger, the offices call for increased education of the public on the long-range implications of social security: the second danger demands that legislation should be so framed as to minimize any tendency to restrict production, and they urge business concerns to 'expand job opportunity among the ageing and handicapped'.

In the United States there are 109 million separate life policies in force among a population of 170 million, and this fact gives added weight to the pronouncements of the life offices in the eyes of the Government. In Great Britain there are 8,780,000 policies among 50 million people, so that the relative figures are 64 per cent in the USA and 17·5 per cent here.

In comparing the situation across the Atlantic with our own, it is impossible to exaggerate what the widespread urge for self-improvement contributes to the American economy. Whereas Europeans still tend to look to politics as the main instrument for social betterment, the American looks to business, and since he was still busy building roads and cities when the Reform Bill was convulsing England, it may be suggested that his country jumped from the eighteenth to the twentieth century in a single bound. No doubt this suggestion needs qualifying, but it is no accident that across the Atlantic business, by and large, attracts abler men than politics. Several ambassadors to this country have been recruited from the ranks of business; Mr Walter S. Gifford was formerly President of the American Telephone and Telegraph Co., Mr Winthrop W. Aldrich held the same office in the Chase National Bank, while the present ambassador, Mr John Whitney, was the senior partner in a Wall Street firm before his appointment to the Court of St James's.

When I first went to America in 1922 to spend a year at Princeton University I saw an advertisement which taught me more economics than any textbook. The picture showed a student shovelling coal into a furnace and the caption read: 'This man may be missing some advantages but he is learning the amount of sweat a ten dollar bill represents'. I had previously been led to expect that Americans would be obsessed with dollars—and of course some of them are—but I soon learned that wealth was very often a measure of character as well as achievement, and represented in American eyes a good deal more than material values.

The emphasis on a man's duty to pay his own way helps to explain the deep misgivings aroused by the fact that for the first time since the Federal Social Security scheme was set up in 1935, the amounts paid in benefits in 1957 exceeded the contributions of the 73 million Americans now covered. As the receipts had been greater than outgoings each year until 1956, the deficit was met from the accrued funds now amounting to $24 billion. The officials responsible for the scheme had expected a temporary drop into the red in 1959, before the next increase in the graded contributions takes effect in 1960, but the earlier deficit was due to over-optimistic calculations when Congress made changes in the Act in 1954 and 1956. As the Federal insurance agency has large sums in hand the whole system is not a burden on the taxpayer, but the deficit has aroused public misgivings and the Government has appointed an independent advisory council to review the long-range financial position. Its report will be no less eagerly read on this side of the Atlantic by all who are concerned that as far as possible the Welfare State should pay its way.

Not very long ago a British Conservative Minister made light of what he termed 'Micawber Economics', implying that the last sixpence in the pound did not matter very much, but to think that we can ignore financial discipline, because eventually the State will provide, is a frame of mind which the City of London will continue to do everything in its power to correct.

11

What We Earn

I sometimes think that those responsible for the business of the City are like pilots; we have to guide the ships of finance and commerce, whatever the international situation and in all political weathers. 'In my time,' said Sir John Braithwaite, speaking as Chairman of the Stock Exchange at a Lord Mayor's banquet, 'the City has disapproved strongly of policies introduced by Liberal, Conservative, Labour and Coalition governments; but it has never failed to give honest cooperation to the Government of the day. I do not think it ever will fail to give that cooperation. But this loyalty is grievously strained when the City as a whole is belittled and its functions distorted and misrepresented; or when the Stock Exchange is abused with unfathomable ignorance and with inexcusable untruth as it has been recently in some sections of the Press.'

Sir John was speaking shortly after the General Election of 1951, when an ex-Minister had gone out of his way to pillory us. Unfortunately, much the same attitude was shown in some quarters during the next General Election in 1955, so much so that *The Times* deplored the 'now largely spurious division of the nation into haves and have nots'. Yet once again, in the autumn of 1957, there was an outburst of extreme feelings against the City in connection with an alleged Bank Rate 'leakage'.

It will be recalled that some large sales of gilt-edged stocks made on the eve of a change in Bank Rate led to the suspicion that certain prominent men had prior knowledge of the change and had used it to private advantage. This led to a demand in Parliament for a public enquiry, and after some hesitation on the part of the Government a reference from the Labour Front Bench to the 'vast City interests' of a prominent Conservative who held an important office in the party brought the whole matter to a head. Many distinguished men in the City were summoned before a tribunal in Westminster Hall presided over by the present Lord Chief Justice, Mr Justice Parker. Evidence was given by, among others, the Chancellor of the Exchequer, and after an exhaustive enquiry lasting several weeks the integrity of all those involved in the City was completely vindicated. Yet this did not serve to silence political criticism, and the Opposition in the House of Commons even voted against accepting the tribunal's report. Making every allowance for the party factor, and the cut and thrust of debate, the speeches revealed a profound ignorance of the City's operations, and there was much confusion as to the precise relations of the Treasury and the Bank of England, although these are now defined by law. Some members seemed to have the fixed idea that the financial operations of the City necessarily clash with the national interest, and *The Economist* said that 'almost alone, Mr Gaitskell, who confined himself to justifying the pressure for an enquiry and criticizing the Government's fumbling, kept clear of this declaration of, in effect, a state of war between Britain's free markets and the Opposition'. The same point was made by *The*

Banker, which, calling on the leaders of the City to explain themselves in face of 'a rising challenge', added that 'the City and Bank must make very sure that their case does not go by default. Much more is involved than a defence of what is traditional: practice must be justified by modern needs.'

While none of us will quickly forget those unhappy weeks, which cast an unnatural gloom over the City, I believe from my own experience in a Yorkshire industrial constituency, which I nursed in the Conservative interest for seven years, that misrepresentation and calumny tend to defeat their object in the fairminded atmosphere which characterises the greater part of political discussion in Britain—certainly outside Parliament, if not always at Westminster itself. In every party there are those who feel deeply and keenly, and it is clearly to the public advantage that all issues should be fully debated. There will always be extremists who are not prepared to reason, but I am personally convinced that the great majority of Englishmen deplore the tendency to distort facts and to attribute false motives to opponents, and that this, more than any other factor, accounts for the apathy often so evident during elections. First and foremost, most people want to hear the facts. If this is so—and I know members of Parliament in all parties who share my view—then the best way to remove the City from the vicious kind of party controversy (as distinct from responsible debate) is to promote the widest possible knowledge of its work and let the facts speak for themselves.

* * * * *

What a remarkable story the City of London has to tell! No other place of business in the world is so steeped in history and romance, and is at the same time so progressive in its methods of finance and communication by which trade all over the world is promoted and developed, with advantage to so many countries besides our own. Institutions and practices that have served us well for centuries still play their part in the City's daily business, side by side with the electronic machines which are invading our offices on an increasing scale. Yet as I asked at the outset of this book, how many people, including some who work in the City, are aware of what we actually earn for the country? Hardly anyone knows much about the 'invisible' earnings which play such an important part in the national housekeeping and affect the daily lives of everyone of us in a vital yet unobtrusive way. The Sterling Area is another topic constantly mentioned in the newspapers, but here again the man in the street has only the vaguest idea of what this remarkable and productive mechanism involves.

Some years ago a letter issued by a firm of stockbrokers to its clients gave such a clear picture of the City's services to the nation that it ought to have been printed in every newspaper in the country. I did, in fact, circulate copies to many editors, although out of respect for the Stock Exchange rule that its members must not advertise, the name of the firm which issued the letter was not included. Unfortunately, the original copy has now been lost, so in reproducing this remarkable document again I can only offer acknowledgments to its competent authors, whoever they may be. It was issued in 1954, but every word of its argument is still valid, so having adapted it by bringing the figures up to date I shall now quote it in full:

'The importance to the British economy of the growing world confidence in sterling is emphasized by the figures of

Britain's balance of payments for 1957. Last year we not only made ends meet, but we did so with a comfortable surplus of £237 million. How was it achieved? Here are the bare bones of the story:

	million
We imported from overseas	£3,605
We exported to other countries	3,508
Leaving a trade deficit of	£97
This was increased by Government overseas expenditure, e.g. Cyprus	143
Giving a total deficit of	£240

Now the invisibles come to the rescue:

	million	
Shipping, on balance, earned us	£115	
Interest on our overseas investments (after deducting interest to our overseas creditors)	100	
Tourists, etc. (a net figure), *minus*	46	
'Others'—to be explained later	308	
		477
Leaving the overall surplus of		£237

'In truth we were saved from bankruptcy by the invisible account. Let us look at these invisibles a little more closely.

'*Shipping*, on balance, brought us £115 million in 1957. This represented the overseas earnings of British tramps and liners (not tankers) over and above our overseas payments for shipping services. Here is the solid contribution which Britain's merchant marine makes to the standard of living in Britain.

'*Interest on Overseas Investments* brought us a net income of

£100 million. This is a shadow of what this income used to be, but the reduction is nothing of which to be ashamed. It reflects the sales of overseas investments that were made in two World Wars so as to provide the financial sinews of war and the weapons of victory. It also reflects the overseas debts incurred by Britain during World War II in fighting the common battle with a financial recklessness which may well have turned the scale of victory in favour of the Allies. Those debts are being promptly and honourably discharged now and in this respect it might be argued that alone of the belligerents—victors and vanquished—Britain is today paying reparations to the rest of the world. The marks which this has left on Britain's net income from overseas investments are, therefore, honourable scars.

'*Tourists, etc.* This small item usually represents a net loss to Britain. This may in due course become a net credit, as more of our dollar-bearing cousins make their way to these islands, where they will always be welcome.

' "*Others.*" Now we come to the really big stuff, an item which on balance brought us £308 million as against £294 in 1956 and only £83 million in 1947. This is the most dynamic item in the British balance of payments. It is a composite item of which the detailed break-down is not published. But the main components are known. They include:

(1) The overseas transactions of *British oil companies*, including tanker earnings. One of the miracles of the balance of payments is the manner in which the effect of trouble in the Middle East has been made good.

(2) *Insurance earnings.* The insurance companies and the Corporation of Lloyds keep the British flag flying

proudly over the greater part of the world. Britain has taught the world the arts of insurance and it still leads the field. Nowhere has this pioneer work been more valuable than in the United States and much of the substantial income which overseas insurance business brings to Britain is remitted here, in good, hard dollars.

(3) *Banking services.* The City of London remains supreme as an international financial centre. About one-half of the world's trade is invoiced and financed in sterling. London's combination of tradition, domestic and overseas banks, acceptance houses and discount market makes up a unique interlocking pattern which many other centres have endeavoured to copy, but none has equalled. The best evidence of the efficacy of this machine is that it should have continued to function so well despite the inconvertibility of sterling. That handicap is being steadily reduced.

(4) *Merchanting services.* These overseas earnings have been mounting as one by one our great commodity markets were freed from the shackles of state trading. Once more British merchants can earn their profits or commissions from transactions in commodities that never even touch these shores. The Ministry of Food could not buy grain in South America and sell it at a profit on the Continent. The trader on the Baltic can do this as a matter of course. Not only do these operations contribute directly to Britain's balance of payments but they do so through all kinds of indirect channels. The transactions in question will probably be financed and insured in London and carried in British ships.

'Thus all these invisibles hang together; but they are suspended from one beam: the strength of sterling and its capacity to earn and hold the confidence of the world.'

At present it holds that confidence; and this is why so large a part of world trade is transacted and financed in sterling. Our currency is used throughout the Sterling Area, which includes all the members of the Commonwealth (except Canada), together with certain countries outside the Commonwealth—Burma, Eire, Iraq, Iceland. All these countries base their currencies on sterling and maintain the bulk of their external reserves in the form of bank balances and other assets in London. Between them and Great Britain, which in effect acts as their banker, there is a close relationship which is of mutual benefit. They have access to all the services which the financial and merchanting institutions of the City of London have to offer, including the London capital market, and, in return, Britain's 'invisible' earnings are swollen.

* * * * *

I have shown how the City's earnings, which amounted to over £300 million in 1957 and are likely to be larger still in 1958,[1] are keeping the national housekeeping 'out of the red', but in view of the sterling crises since the war some people are asking whether the Sterling Area matters as much to the country as the figures suggest. This question is so important for the future that I propose to seek the aid of an expert in answering it and to quote briefly from Mr William Clarke's book, *The City's Invisible Earnings*, published in October, 1958 by the Institute of Economic Affairs. I would also refer

[1] A statement for the first six months of 1958, prepared while this book was in proof, will be found on page 150.

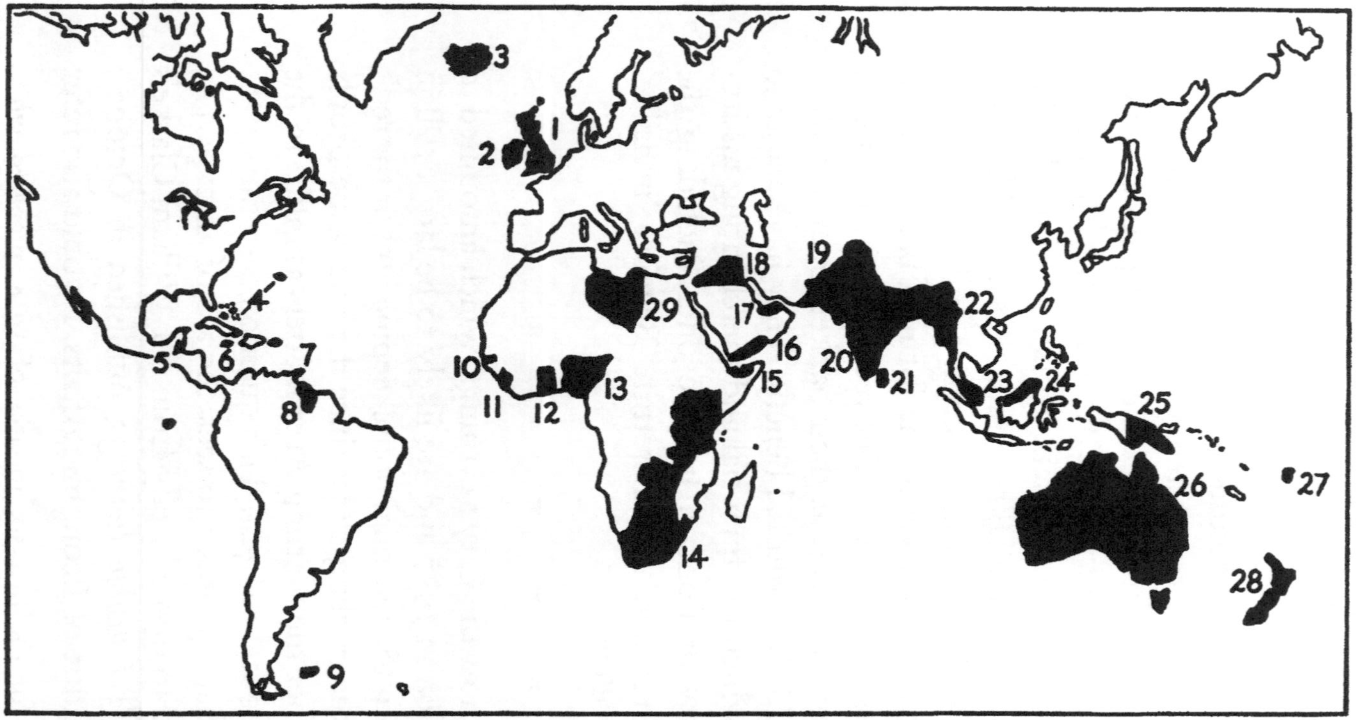

The Sterling Area (marked in black on this map) comprises a great variety of countries, including: 1, The United Kingdom; 2, Ireland; 3, Iceland; 4, Bermuda and Bahamas; 5, British Honduras; 6, Jamaica; 7, Barbados and Trinidad; 8, British Guiana; 9, Falkland Islands and dependencies; 10, Gambia; 11, Sierra Leone; 12, Ghana; 13. Nigeria; 14, Union of South Africa and African dependencies; 15, British Somaliland; 16, Aden; 17, Trucial Oman, Bahrein and Qatar; 18, Iraq, Jordan and Kuwait; 19, Pakistan; 20, India; 21, Ceylon; 22, Burma; 23, Federation of Malaya; 24, British North Borneo; 25, New Guinea; 26, Australia; 27, Fiji; 28, New Zealand; 29, Libya.

the reader to Mr Paul Bareau's *The Future of the Sterling System*, issued by the same Institute.

Mr Clarke, who is City Editor of *The Times*, points out that as the crisis in the autumn of 1957 occurred at a time when the United Kingdom was running a comfortable surplus on the balance of payments, it has been suggested that we should do well to opt out of the sterling system and curtail our commitments as an international banker. It has also been alleged that the loss of income to the City would be less than many people fear. In reply to these suggestions, the first answer is that a good share of the City's total earnings is attracted here because Britain is acting as an international banker and clearing house, and many of these earnings depend on the ease with which payments can be settled throughout the world. The idea that the greater part of the City's invisible income would remain intact if the use of sterling were restricted is far from the mark. Secondly, since the abdication of our role would mean freezing our outstanding sterling liabilities of some £4,000 million, any Government is, fortunately, most unlikely to take this drastic step. In the third place, if London no longer financed international trade, it is difficult to see which other centre would be able to do so. New York is hardly equipped to take on international business on this scale, and for various technical reasons our role could not be assumed by Zurich or Amsterdam.

'The figures of the City's earnings speak for themselves,' Mr Clarke concludes. 'But the true measure of the City's value is not just this invisible income. . . . London is still providing the mechanism for a large share of the world's finance and commerce. Surprising as it may seem in a decade in which the pound has remained officially inconvertible, no other financial centre has even attempted to take over the mantle from London. While this is not an altruistic role, the City does play an invaluable part in creating a truly international society in which commercial cooperation and economic interdependence loom larger than national rivalries. In addition to the fees and commissions from their services, these institutions are also providing the basis on which the United Kingdom can develop an expanding multilateral trade with the rest of the world. It is basically on these grounds rather than on the size of its invisible earnings, large as they are, that the City of London fulfils itself.'

More than ever today, what we earn for the country is indispensable to the nation. But to the mass of the people the City is still a closed book, and in a final chapter I shall suggest ways and means for filling a dangerous and quite unnecessary gap in our armour.

12

A Time to Speak

Enough has been said in this book to show that the City of London is a very busy place, and that most of those who work there are occupied with transactions which call for immediate and detailed attention. I have tried to explain that we deal with money in much the same way that a grocer handles currants, and that the profits and losses which occur at one time or another in the City, as in other places of business, do not strike us as in any way unusual. They are a measure of what we are doing, whether in banking or insurance or stockbroking or in the commodity markets. When, therefore, our work is criticized, as if it were in some way different from any other, it comes as a surprise and shock to most of those who are 'Something in the City'. That politics in a democracy should be concerned with finance and economics is, of course, right and proper: and the memory that the return to the Gold Standard in the nineteen-twenties was followed by heavy unemployment still arouses deep feelings. But in view of the great changes in political thinking since the war, and the acceptance of full employment by all parties, the attacks still made on the City of London suggest that there is a tremendous need to promote a better understanding of our work at Westminster, and that this is also a time to speak to the people.

On the principle that charity begins at home, I believe that steps to make the City's vital contribution to the national housekeeping better known should start in our own ranks. Nearly every City firm has opportunities to tell its staff and shareholders and customers how its operations fit into the wider picture. Leaflets, newsletters, staff magazines and press advertising can all be used for this purpose, and of course the Annual Report offers a great opportunity to take everyone concerned 'behind the scenes'. Such action is entirely in the hands of the firm, it can be quickly effected and does not involve the compromises and delay which collective advertising on the part of several firms is apt to entail. In publishing facts about the work of the City, there is a parallel opportunity to help people to understand what keeps the wheels of business of all kinds turning: an advertisement dealing with overseas earnings, for example, can also be made to illustrate the basic principle that, like the nation itself, every commercial undertaking must pay its way or go under.

It is fairly easy to understand what a coal miner does: we all use his product, we all realize that mining is a dangerous trade and so the miner rightly commands the popular respect. It is far less easy to understand that a City worker is equally productive, yet a wider appreciation of this would be a spur to all of us, whether we go to work in cloth caps or bowler hats.

For centuries the world-wide activities of the City of London have depended on personal character and initiative, which have been its driving force in the service of the private firm, the public company and latterly of the State-controlled undertaking. The City is accustomed to take the long view and is acutely aware that this driving force must be preserved and actively encouraged, whatever the colour of the Government or the structure of an industry may be. The campaign I am suggesting is not, therefore, an attempt to preserve the *status quo*—that can never be done for very long. It is not a veiled attempt to 'keep the socialists out'—as Her Majesty's opposition the Labour Party is the alternative government. While first promoting the well-being of the City, the campaign could also bring about a wider understanding of what keeps our free society going.

For the particular firm, just as for the nation, the need to balance the budget, to keep business units within manageable size, and to compete on economic terms will always be imperative. On the personal side, hard work and common sense, individual initiative and responsibility, quick decisions at all levels, fair dealing and a sense of service—these are similar factors on which the prosperity of Britain will continue to depend. I believe that advertising designed to high-light these factors, if carried out on a wide enough scale, can do much to solve economic problems and to foster social content. Up to now, more has been done along these lines by industrial firms than by those in the City, so that the examples to be mentioned in this chapter are mainly from sources outside. In referring to just a few firms I realize that many others are also doing admirable work. Even so, taking British enterprise as a whole, this kind of publicity is still in its infancy; and in the case of the City, for every firm which is alive to the pressing need to make its business better known, dozens are still working in silence.

* * * * *

For the popular impression that capitalist enterprise is only interested in making money I believe that lack of publicity is very largely to blame. Nor are the reports we do issue always designed to put our work in the right perspective. It is still possible to read a company report in the newspaper which makes no reference to the business or trade of the firm concerned. Naturally, the shareholder wants to know what is happening to his money and the emphasis on finance at company meetings is entirely natural and proper. But unless reference is also made to the work from which the profits or losses arise, the popular impression is created that only the money matters. The practice of heading a report with an explanatory line under the name of the company (e.g. James Smith and Sons Ltd., welding machine makers) is growing, but as late as August, 1958 a report was published by an engineering concern in a London newspaper without a single line to show what its products were or where they were sold.

This brings me to some examples of the opposite kind. Another engineering firm, for instance, recently had a good attendance of shareholders at an 'at home' given by the directors to coincide with the annual meeting. A special train was run from London, and they were able to see at first hand how their money was being used in making radio receivers, to the advantage of the public, the employees and the shareholders. It follows that such firms are keeping their staffs posted on the value of the daily job, showing how each process contributes to the finished product and the product in turn to the national need. The importance of cooperation, and how good team work leads to better output, was the subject of some striking advertisements which John Laing & Son, Ltd., the civil engineers and contractors, published 'to show what British workers can achieve in spite of difficulties, given opportunity and backed by enterprise'.

The erection of a new television station in the Pennines, 1,750 feet above sea-level, involved working in swirling cloud and sometimes drenching rain, the stones having to be hacked out of the snow and thawed over coke-braziers. 'The men never gave in. They not only finished the work on time; they made a good job of it. They worked with a will and they worked as a team.' This kind of advertising, which is also used effectively by the Taylor Woodrow organization, serves the double purpose of enhancing the prestige of a particular firm and at the same time giving a fillip to national morale. I recall another example, which put in a word for British technology in connection with exports. The advertisement explained how the problem of 'cargo-sweat', which disfigured the bodywork and upholstery of motor-cars in transit through tropical seas, was solved by paint-research chemists, 'thus helping a British car-manufacturer to maintain a valuable export market in Australia'.

A big firm with interests in the United States, Borax Consolidated Ltd., issues regular newsletters to its shareholders to keep them posted on commercial and technical developments. Some very good advertising has been undertaken by the British Electricity Authority to show how new power stations built since the war are meeting an ever-growing demand. Similar themes have been used by Associated Electrical Industries. A typical advertisement opened with a statement by the chairman, Lord Chandos, which read: 'Electrical power is now one of the essentials of any developing community, and the standard of living, particularly in this country, depends on our ensuring that we keep abreast of the demand'. The same announcement explained how income was spent, and also referred to overseas orders, the company's expansion programme, and its research policy—including the need to recruit the right men to serve the company in the future. Appropriately, a big canvas is also used by the P. & O. shipping company, whose chairman, Sir William Currie, never hesitates to comment in its announcements on current issues affecting shipping. Maps are often included to show the far-flung routes of the P. & O. fleet and, as befits a great business with headquarters in the City of London, attention is drawn to the important role of the company in maintaining and improving shipping services.

The question, however, may properly be asked whether publicity of this kind can ever make much impression on the British public, since even the resources at the disposal of modern governments barely sufficed to bring home, for example, the gravity of inflation. I believe there are at least two answers. In the first place the surface of public opinion has barely been scratched by serious publicity designed to explain economic issues in simple terms. Secondly, a distinction must be made between advertising mass-produced articles and publicity relating to economic issues, which calls for an approach in the first place to the thinking minority of all political persuasions, whose influence is out of all proportion to their numbers. Many of these are the floating voters, who are estimated to comprise at least 10 per cent of the electorate. They are the folk who chip in when a speaker is getting too far from the facts, whether at a meeting, in a railway carriage or in a bar. Yet I think we must not underrate the sound judgment and common sense of the public at large, provided the facts are fully and fairly presented and that the appeal is made on a high enough note. The true Englishman, whatever his politics, is deeply concerned about the recurrent crises which we have so often faced since the war, and does not wish to see party capital made out of the nation's difficulties. Those who are doubtful about his judgment may take comfort from a saying attributed to Sir Winston Churchill, that 'Democracy is the worst form of government—except the others'. Another remark, this one from a famous American statesman, is also relevant. 'I know of no safe depository,' said Thomas Jefferson, 'of the ultimate powers of society but the people themselves; and if we think of them as not enlightened enough to exercise their control with a wholesome discretion, the remedy is not to take it from them, but to inform their discretion by education.'

* * * * *

Besides publicity by each and every firm on its own account, I believe that the overall picture of the City's services and earnings calls for collective efforts if an adequate impression is to be made. *The City Press*, edited by Mr S. W. Alexander, is a vigorous ambassador for our work and institutions. Valuable work is also being done by the City of London Society through films and lectures, and the Institute of Economic Affairs is now publishing some excellent books, but in addition something really arresting is required to catch and hold the public eye. Lloyds Bank prints in the newspapers a statement headed 'An Account of Stewardship', showing how its resources are disposed, and from time to time Sir Oliver Franks explains the true significance of banking figures to the public. A similar statement of the City's earnings (see page 150) should be issued at frequent intervals, and put before the public by every means that modern communications can offer. Press advertising on a wide scale could be extended by many other methods, including of course television. The

WHAT THE CITY OF LONDON EARNED FOR BRITAIN'S OVERSEAS PAYMENTS

JANUARY–JUNE 1958

British merchandise ('visible') overseas trade:—

	millions		*millions*
Exports to other countries	£1,753	Imports into the United Kingdom	£1,616
		Visible trade surplus	137
	£1,753		£1,753

This was the first time on record that the United Kingdom had a surplus in its merchandise trade alone in any six month period.

The City of London's ('invisible') earnings helped to swell this surplus and to meet the British Government's overseas expenditure and the deficit on tourist trade:—

	millions		*millions*
Shipping (net)	£82	Government overseas expenditure	£100
Interest on overseas investments (net)	40	Tourists and emigrants' remittances (net loss to Britain)	5
Insurance, banking, merchanting	180	Invisible trade surplus	197
	£302		£302

The total surplus of £334 millions on Britain's overseas account from January-June 1958 was the largest ever achieved in the first six months of any year.

figures could be supplemented by brief explanations of such topics as invisible earnings, and gradually a picture could be built up in the public mind of the City of London as an indispensable national institution.

I should like to see the banks, the insurance companies, the shipping lines and all the leading institutions combining in a collective campaign, which should be designed to give information about all aspects of our work, somewhat on the lines which are being so successfully used by the 'Operation Britain' organization for publicising the achievements of the nation at large. A start should be made with the City's earnings, as the central feature, since the figures speak for themselves and if made widely known in bold and simple terms, could not fail to impress the public.

Several attempts since the war to promote collective advertising have lacked adequate support. Some influential people have felt that it might only encourage controversy of the wrong kind and that it would be a mistake for the City to 'answer back'. I must therefore emphasize that the campaign I envisage would be purely factual, and that any statements of a political nature, such as may be called for when particular trades or services are criticized on party platforms or in Parliament, would remain with particular trade organizations. For example, when industrial assurance was suggested as a candidate for nationalization, the companies undertook a campaign to put their case. Had the City's statement of earnings been a *fait accompli* at that time, it would have included figures for insurance, but would not have added any comment on the political issues then in the public eye. The City's traditional dislike of advertising is not due only to an aversion to any form of boasting but dates back to the days when its supremacy in finance and international commerce was unchallenged at home as well as abroad. It is not, I think, untrue to suggest that its leading position is now better recognized overseas than in our own country; and in view of the political attitude disclosed during the proceedings of the Bank Rate Tribunal, many who were previously opposed to publicity for the City have changed their minds in the light of the ignorance and prejudice displayed. Nevertheless, what we now need is leadership of a kind which, as Mr Henry Ford II once said, 'acts rather than reacts, seizes the initiative, and moves ahead by design rather than in response to outside pressures.'

It is encouraging to note that the Governor of the Bank of England has appeared on radio and television, and is making speeches to show that—in his own phrase—the 'old Lady of Threadneedle Street is very much up to date'. Much pioneer work of this kind has been done by Sir John Braithwaite, who continues to give addresses on the Stock Exchange to schools and popular audiences all over the country. Similar efforts are being made by some other leaders in the City, which has a new and powerful advocate in Lord Monckton, but much more work of this kind is needed and could do an immense amount of good, side by side with intensive publicity by individual firms. But I believe that the value of all these steps would be far greater against the background of the City's earnings made known by a sustained collective campaign, through which the City of London would speak to the people with a united voice.

At no time has the City been better fitted to carry out its immense and varied tasks. At home, we are enjoying a new lease of freedom and renewed vigour after the inevitable restrictions of the war; abroad, we are gaining fresh ground with advantage to the country and the world; and the prospect of convertible sterling and developments in Europe open up further vistas. The tremendous wave of building now transforming the face of the City, and the installation of scientific devices on an increasing scale, attest to our confidence in the future and to our belief that Parliament will continue to uphold our traditional liberties. Above all, a new generation is getting into its stride and is mastering the special techniques to which our position as the financial centre of the world is so largely due. It is now up to us to tell the people what the City of London will continue to mean to our great trading nation in the promising years ahead.

THE END